# VICTORIOUS
# CHRISTIAN
# LIVING

# ALAN REDPATH

# VICTORIOUS CHRISTIAN LIVING

## STUDIES IN THE BOOK OF JOSHUA

Fleming H. Revell
A Division of Baker Book House Co
Grand Rapids, Michigan 49516

©1955, 1993 by Fleming H. Revell

Published by Fleming H. Revell,
a division of Baker Book House Company
P.O. Box 6287, Grand Rapids, Michigan 49516-6287

ISBN: 0-8007-5490-5

Printed in the United States of America

TO THE CONGREGATIONS OF

THE MOODY MEMORIAL CHURCH, CHICAGO
and
DUKE STREET CHURCH, RICHMOND, SURREY, ENGLAND

*to whose infinite patience, love and prayers
I owe so much.*

# CONTENTS

8                 CONTENTS

## PART III   LIVING THE LIFE

# INTRODUCTION

PAUL S. REES

To THOSE WHO HAVE NEVER HEARD ALAN REDPATH PREACH let me say that he is no "reed shaken with the wind." It would be more accurate to say that he is an oak swept by a gale. The sheer bigness of the Gospel blows cleanly and powerfully through his soul.

Unlike many a preacher—many a good preacher indeed—he has a grasp of the *wholeness* of the message of the New Testament—and of the previews of that message in the Old Testament. We say to the unconverted: "Trust Christ!" We say to the struggling, often-frustrated, Christian: "Try harder! Pray more! Strive onward! Give yourself time!"

What is missing? All the wealth of God's Word as touching the Holy Spirit—the gift of power! It doesn't cancel discipline; it only rescues it from drudgery and defeat!

Here, in these throbbing pages, is the message of robust and radiant living. It is set within the context of that dramatic document of Holy Writ—the Book of Joshua.

Not every reader will give unqualified approval to every turn of phrase or every doctrinal implication, but none can fail, I should suppose, to be probed and profited by the author's central message. Gentle hint to the reader: it's better to be a *consumer of truth* than to be a *connoisseur of terms*.

It is the passion for Christlike living that I have seen flaming in Alan Redpath's ministry. That flame kindles me. It may well have the same effect on *you*.

Not theological "Big Berthas" but spiritual "flame throwers"—that's what these pages are!

# FOREWORD

THE BEST WAY TO VINDICATE THE WORD OF GOD IS TO preach it. Every page, from the opening verses of Genesis to the closing verses of Revelation, shows the watermark of heavenly authenticity. Every page is, of course, both historically and scientifically accurate. While, however, the Bible has been proved to be all this, it is not primarily a book of history, nor is it primarily a book of scientific record. First and foremost, it is a book of Divine revelation. The whole Book is a complete revelation of God's plan of redemption for mankind. He places it in our hands as the key which unlocks the mystery of His love, of our sin, of His justice and mercy, and of His program of salvation.

Once we regard the Bible as a whole it begins to take on a new meaning. The Old Testament is preparatory to the New. The New cannot be understood apart from the Old, nor can the Old be appreciated apart from the New. Furthermore, we begin to discover that God's way of dealing with man in the Old Testament is but a picture of His dealing with man in the New. Salvation for a fallen race was to be through the Man Christ Jesus from the very beginning; but prior to His coming, His death and resurrection, God dealt with the nation into whom Christ was to be born in the same way as He would thereafter deal with men individually through the Lord Jesus Christ. In other words, God's dealing with Israel was a type of His dealings with you and me.

Once we grasp that truth the Old Testament is transformed from a book of dry history and unintelligible sacrifices into a book of Divine revelation. This is particularly true of the book of Joshua, which we are about to study. Within its pages, I believe, we shall find the secret of so much that is lacking in Christian experience today.

It has been my profound conviction for some years now that the greatest need of the Christian Church is a revival of the New Testament standard of Christian living. There seems to be a very wide gulf between what we believe and how we live, a marked contrast between our position in Christ and our actual experience. Too often do we claim to believe our Bible from cover to cover, but fail to live out its truths in daily conduct. Before we can ever see a real movement of the Spirit of God in blessing to the world in our day, surely the church must face afresh the New Testament pattern, the whole revelation of the Word of God, in its claims on holiness of life and ethical conduct.

The fact is that in conservative evangelical circles today there is a great deal of propaganda and program, talent and testimony, but too little progress in bringing our generation to the Lord. The way of real blessing is costly, often unspectacular, always fruitful. This book is written with the fervent prayer and desire that, somehow, the Lord may use it for His glory to help many people to face afresh the implications of the Cross and the pattern of God's redemption in personal life. Victorious Christian living can be not only a theory to be admired, but also an experience to be enjoyed.

Much of the subject matter of this book was preached in

the Moody Church pulpit over a period of six months at the commencement of my ministry there in September, 1953. It was at the request of a number of the congregation that I decided to put these messages in printed form, retaining in the main the structure of the messages as preached, revising only where it seemed necessary for easier reading. I trust that the reader with a critical eye will bear that in mind, and be merciful!

I owe a great deal, not only in my personal life, but in my reading and in the preparation of this book, to the writings of Dr. F. B. Meyer and Dr. Graham Scroggie, both of whom preached, wrote, and lived the victorious Christian life, and whose ministries have been a profound blessing, not only to myself, but to countless thousands of others. It is my earnest prayer that what the Lord has taught me, not only through His Word, but through these His servants, may be imparted by these pages to bring blessing to many more.

I would like to express my grateful thanks to Miss Arline Harris for her painstaking and efficient work in the preparation and correction of the manuscript.

*Chicago, Ill.*                                             **A. R.**

# PART I

*Facing the Objective*

# CHAPTER 1

# THE GOAL OF CHRISTIAN LIVING

### JOSHUA 1:2

*Now after the death of Moses the servant of the Lord it came to pass, that the Lord spake unto Joshua the son of Nun, Moses' minister, saying,*

*Moses my servant is dead; now therefore arise, go over this Jordan, thou, and all this people, unto the land which I do give to them, even to the children of Israel.*

*Every place that the sole of your foot shall tread upon, that have I given unto you, as I said unto Moses.*

*From the wilderness and this Lebanon even unto the great river, the river Euphrates, all the land of the Hittites, and unto the great sea toward the going down of the sun, shall be your coast.*

*There shall not any man be able to stand before thee all the days of thy life: as I was with Moses, so I will be with thee: I will not fail thee, nor forsake thee.*

*Be strong and of a good courage: for unto this people shalt thou divide for an inheritance the land, which I sware unto their fathers to give them.*

*Only be thou strong and very courageous, that thou mayest observe to do according to all the law, which Moses my servant commanded thee: turn not from it to the right hand or to the left, that thou mayest prosper whithersoever thou goest.*

*This book of the law shall not depart out of thy mouth; but thou shalt meditate therein day and night, that thou mayest observe to do according to all that is written therein: for then thou shalt make thy way prosperous, and then thou shalt have good success.*

*Have not I commanded thee? Be strong and of good courage; be not afraid, neither be thou dismayed: for the Lord thy God is with thee whithersoever thou goest.*

A casual reading of the book of Joshua might well cause us to question why so much place has been given in the Word of God to a record of the military victories of Joshua and his army in the conquest of the land of Canaan. There surely must be an inner meaning to this book which is not discovered at first sight.

In our search for that inner meaning we might well be sidetracked by some of our hymnology, for in so many hymns Jordan is an illustration of death and Canaan of heaven. If we apply that meaning to the book of Joshua, then there can be no explanation whatsoever of the many incidents recorded in its pages. Here we discover that Canaan is a place of warfare. Surely this cannot be the portion of those who have entered their rest. The Christian has an enemy with whom to contend during all his earthly experience, but he eagerly waits for the day when his battles will be over and he will be in the presence of his Lord. No, we must look further if we are really to understand what lies behind the historical record of these twenty-four chapters.

I would suggest that the clue to the interpretation of this

Old Testament book is found in the epistle to the Ephesians and in the epistle to the Hebrews. For example, in the third and fourth chapters of Hebrews we find that the land of Canaan is a picture of the spiritual rest and victory which may be enjoyed here on earth by every believer, a rest of faith in the Lord Jesus Christ. Again, the Ephesian letter speaks of life "in the heavenly places"—not in heaven, but in the experience of oneness with our Risen Lord in His victory here and now, the place of the fullness of God's blessing. I believe that we shall understand the real significance of the book of Joshua only if we recognize that what it is in the Old Testament the epistle to the Ephesians is in the New. This suggestion, of course, has to be substantiated from the Word of God itself.

Therefore, as in this opening chapter we survey the book and its meaning as a whole, I want you to think of the analogy between the land of Canaan and the land of full salvation which is the portion of every believer in the Lord Jesus Christ.

First of all, we realize that Canaan was the goal to which God was leading His people. When He appeared to Moses in the burning bush, He pledged Himself not only to deliver the Israelites from the bondage of Egypt, but also to bring them into a land flowing with milk and honey:

And the Lord said, I have surely seen the affliction of my people which are in Egypt, and have heard their cry by reason of their taskmasters; for I know their sorrows; and I am come down to deliver them out of the hand of the Egyptians, and to bring them up out of that land unto a good land and a large, unto a land flowing with milk and honey; unto the place of the Canaanites, and the Hittites, and the Amo-

rites, and the Perizzites, and the Hivites, and the Jebusites
(Ex. 3:7, 8).

In other words, the deliverance from Egypt was only in
preparation for the enjoyment of Canaan. The passover, the
shedding of the blood, the crossing of the Red Sea, the destruction of Pharoah's hosts, all would have been useless unless they led to the place of rest in Canaan. Furthermore, it
was only by possession of the land of Canaan that the promise
of God to Abraham could be fulfilled.

And the Lord said unto Abram, after that Lot was separated from him, Lift up now thine eyes, and look from the
place where thou art northward, and southward, and eastward, and westward: for all the land which thou seest, to
thee will I give it, and to thy seed forever. And I will make
thy seed as the dust of the earth: so that if a man can number
the dust of the earth, then shall thy seed also be numbered.
Arise, walk through the land in the length of it and in the
breadth of it; for I will give it unto thee (Gen. 14:13-17).

Is it not also true that the greatest passages in the New
Testament are written, not so much for the conversion of
the sinner, but for the perfecting of the saint, and for revealing the way of true holiness of life? The foundations of our
faith—regeneration and justification—are deeply laid in order
that they may carry the superstructure of sanctification and
holiness. As Paul said in Romans 8:30, "Moreover whom he
did predestinate, them he also called: and whom he called,
them he also justified: and whom he justified, them he also
glorified." We were redeemed that we might be His purchased possession; justified that we might be sanctified and
glorified. We were brought out that we might be brought in.

Yet is it not true that the majority of Christians come far short, and are content with a wilderness experience—justified, but not enjoying the possession of all their inheritance in Christ? My dear readers, at the very outset of your consideration of this book, I ask you to consider carefully your own spiritual experience. Are you in the wilderness of defeat, or in the land of victory? Is your life a constant struggle against the powers of darkness, with constant defeat, or is it a victorious war waged in the power of a Risen Lord?

Furthermore, observe, from the opening verses of the first chapter of the book of Joshua, that it was impossible for the law to lead into the land of Canaan: "Moses, my servant, is dead; now therefore arise, go over this Jordan." The law could never inherit God's promises, not because there was any defect in the law (you will remember that Moses was the representative of the law, and when he died his natural force was unabated and his eye undimmed), but the law could not inherit the promises of God because of human infirmity and sin.

In Romans 7, which I believe to be the experience of a regenerate man, Paul acclaims the law of God as just and holy, but acknowledges the existence of another law in his members warring against the law of God. The presence of this evil law in us makes it impossible to fulfill God's law and to enter into His full blessing. We do not attain the full rest and victory of Christian experience by our resolution or by our consecration, or even by praying and fasting. We shall see, however, that such blessing is bestowed on all who, in the absence of all merit and effort, receive it with open and empty hands of faith. The Christian does not work up toward victory, he works down from it. We do not struggle toward it, but we stand in it because of the Cross and an empty tomb.

Again, you will observe that entrance into the land of Canaan was entrusted to a representative. God repeatedly addressed Joshua and bestowed on him what was intended for the people, "Go over this Jordan, thou, and all this people" (Joshua 1:2). So everything in Canaan was put into the hands of Joshua as trustee for the people. It was his responsibility to divide and assign the land as each tribe came to claim its portion from him.

How perfectly this is fulfilled in the Lord Jesus Christ! To him all spiritual blessing has been given, and He holds it in trust for us to claim. God has nothing for any one of us except we find it in the Lord Jesus Christ. All power was given unto Him, that He might give us authority over the power of the devil. The Lord Jesus Christ is full of grace and truth, that out of His fullness we might all receive. He received the promise of the Holy Spirit, that He might pour Himself forth in pentecostal power on us. Whatever He has is held in trust for us, to be bestowed as by faith we claim our inheritance.

Observe the third and fourth verses of Joshua 1: "Every place that the sole of your foot shall tread upon, that have I given unto you." The whole land was given to the people, but they could possess only the portion which they claimed. We must not only know our title, but make our claim to every blessing. The greatest of saints are the greatest receivers. Let us believe that we receive, reckon on it, and live in the power of it, and so act on faith. All of the Lord Jesus Christ is mine at the moment of conversion, but I possess only as much of Him as by faith I claim.

To continue the analogy, you will observe that a whole

generation died in the wilderness before the land of Canaan was attained. Only Joshua and Caleb of the generation which left Egypt succeeded in entering the land. These things happen yet; indeed, this is the story of the Christian Church today. Surely the state of the church must be a sorrow to the heart of God. In spite of Calvary, in spite of an empty tomb and an ascended Lord, in spite of Pentecost, the majority of Christians perish in indulgence, worldliness, and sin. "Saved," as the Apostle Paul says, "but as by fire."

Only here and there do we find a Joshua or a Caleb "who wholly followed the Lord." Yet His word to us all still is, "Go over this Jordan, thou, and all this people."

Of course, there is a reason why the church does not press in to the land of blessing. Our analogy holds yet further when we remember that Canaan was inhabited by strong enemies. Seven nations held the land of Canaan with strongholds and chariots of iron, and the land of full salvation in the Lord Jesus Christ is certainly not free from conflict or from the presence of foes. That dramatic chapter which illustrates so perfectly the spiritual warfare of the saints, in Ephesians 6, reminds us that "we wrestle not against flesh and blood, but against principalities, against powers, against the rulers of the darkness of this world, against spiritual wickedness in high places. Wherefore take unto you the whole armour of God, that ye may be able to withstand in the evil day, and having done all, to stand."

Full blessing in the Christian life is not bestowed except to eager, hungry people who press in to receive it. True, God has blessed us with all spiritual blessings in heavenly places in Christ, but the blessing is in heavenly places, and these are places to which Satan has access, and where he can still cast all his fiery darts. God does not bless His child unless He sees him eager for the blessing. He does not pour out of His fullness on a plate, as it were, and invite us to help ourselves at a low level of expectancy. He desires every one of His children to press in against all the assaults of the enemy, that we may lay hold of that which is our inheritance in the Lord Jesus Christ, knowing that every foe we shall ever meet in that battle already has been met and conquered by our Joshua.

Therefore, from these analogies which I have drawn I think you will see that this book of Joshua will open up for us what will be, to many people, new areas in God's plan of redemption for us all, new possibilities of spiritual victory, new secrets of the way of blessing. This book of Joshua will cease to be, if indeed it is now to any of my readers, a mere record of historic events, and will become a revelation of what God can do in and through the life that is utterly yielded to Him

# CHAPTER 2

# THE MAN GOD USES

## JOSHUA 1:9

*Then Joshua commanded the officers of the people, saying,*
*Pass through the host, and command the people, saying,*
*Prepare you victuals; for within three days ye shall pass over*
*this Jordan, to go in to possess the land, which the Lord your*
*God giveth you to possess it.*

*And to the Reubenites, and the Gadites, and to half the*
*tribe of Manasseh, spake Joshua, saying,*

*Remember the word which Moses the servant of the Lord*
*commanded you, saying, The Lord your God hath given*
*you rest, and hath given you this land.*

*Your wives, your little ones, and your cattle, shall remain*
*in the land which Moses gave you on this side Jordan; but ye*
*shall pass before your brethren armed, all the mighty men of*
*valour, and help them;*

*Until the Lord have given your brethren rest, as he hath*
*given you, and they also have possessed the land which the*
*Lord your God giveth them: then ye shall return unto the*
*land of your possession, and enjoy it, which Moses the Lord's*
*servant gave you on this side Jordan toward the sunrising.*

*And they answered Joshua, saying, All that thou com-*

*mandest us we will do, and whithersoever thou sendest us,*
*we will go.*

*According as we hearkened unto Moses in all things, so*
*will we hearken unto thee: only the Lord thy God be with*
*thee, as he was with Moses.*

*Whosoever he be that doth rebel against thy command-*
*ment, and will not hearken unto thy words in all that thou*
*commandest him, he shall be put to death: only be strong*
*and of a good courage.*

JOSHUA 1:10–18

We have begun by thinking about the inner meaning of this
book of Joshua. The command of God was, "Go over this
Jordan, thou, and all this people, unto the land which I do
give to them." This opened up before us the possibility of
life on a higher plane, deliverance from a wilderness experience of defeat into the experience of victory, even though it
be through warfare and conflict.

I am sure that in the hearts of all of us there is the cry,
"How can I be a person whom God can use?" What sort of
person does God entrust with spiritual leadership? Let us
think for a moment of the leader whom God appointed,
Joshua. On the threshold of this new era of responsibility,
God's word to Joshua was, "Have I not commanded thee? Be
strong and of a good courage; be not afraid, neither be thou
dismayed: for the Lord thy God is with thee whithersoever
thou goest" (Joshua 1:9).

Does that mean that all of us have to be strong if we are to
lead God's work? If so, there is little hope for any of us.
As did Paul, we often cry, "Who is sufficient for these
things?" Yet not once but many times God spoke to Joshua
and said, "Be strong." Why? Surely because Joshua was

conscious of his inadequacy and of his weakness. He never thought that such an honor would be conferred on him. He was perfectly content to play second fiddle, and to be Moses' servant and minister. But one day the call came, and his heart failed him.

God said, "Be strong," and when God said that it meant that the man to whom He spoke felt weak. God said, "Be not afraid," which meant that the man to whom He spoke was frightened. God said, "Neither be thou dismayed," which meant that the man to whom God spoke would easily quit the job altogether. But when men feel like that, God comes and lifts them up to leadership and into responsibility.

Most of us, God forgive us, are too big for God to use. We are too full of our own schemes and of our own way of doing things. God has to humble us and break us and empty us. So low, indeed, must God make us that we need every word of encouragement from heaven to enable us to take on the job and dare to go forward in the will of God. The world speaks about the survival of the fittest, but God gives power to the faint and He gives might to those who have no strength. He perfects His strength in weakness; He uses the things that are not to bring to nought the things that are. If Paul had been as eloquent as he confessed himself to be contemptible in speech, he could never have become the great apostle.

Consider with me, then, three sources of Joshua's strength as a leader of God's people. First of all, I would ask you to observe that here is *a faithful man.* Verse one of this chapter mentions that Joshua was Moses' minister. What a wonderful word in the Book that word "minister" is. In Britain we often use "minister" instead of "pastor." A minister is one who is prepared, not to domineer over people, but to serve them for

Jesus' sake. Faithfulness in a few things is always demanded as a condition for ruling over many things.

If Josephus the historian is accurate, Joshua had lived for forty years in bondage to Egypt. He had known the hardship, the frustration, the cruelty, the intolerance of the taskmasters. For forty more years he had patiently endured the wanderings in the wilderness. In the course of that journey he had fought with and defeated the enemies of God's people, the Amalekites. Joshua had gone into the Promised Land, and he had returned with a minority report. He had seen the giants, but he believed his God was able. And after Joshua's eighty years of faithful service behind the scenes, suddenly God speaks to him and bids him assume the position of leadership of this mighty army.

Who can tell today for what God is preparing us? So often we murmur at the narrow round of daily duty. So often we think we are worthy of something bigger. Our little sphere of service seems so inadequate and so unworthy. But I want to say to you that every hour of it is essential if God would make you a man He can use.

We must suffer if we would reign. We must descend before we ascend. God's will for a man's life never comes through the big things but through the little things. If we meet the smallest responsibility, dignify the smallest duty with the most response of our mind and heart and personality, one day God will relieve us of the little thing and give us a big thing to do.

In the kitchen of a little apartment in London the wife of a friend of mine has a little motto over the kitchen sink which reads like this: "Divine service is conducted here three times daily." I think there is a breath of heaven about that. It is our faithfulness in these small things that enables us to be men whom, some day, God can trust with big things.

But if that be the qualification for leadership, we had better resign right now. None of us has always done the things that nobody can see as thoroughly as the things that everybody watches. We have all sought to serve God at some time or other because of what we think we get out of it, wretched men that we are. We dare not face the future and claim that we have been faithful in the past. Shall we resign? Oh, no, wait a moment.

Joshua was but a shadow; our Lord Jesus Christ is the reality. When Jesus emerged from obscurity He had put in thirty years of preparation—for just three years of ministry. He was subject to His parents, He knew the discipline of His home, He dignified hard work by laboring as a carpenter in Nazareth. Nothing imperfect was ever turned out of that shop. Jesus attended a local church every Sunday, and, if I may say so, a dead church at that. He lived in a home where His whole outlook was utterly misunderstood in His own family circle.

But one day He stepped out of obscurity, was baptized, and entered into His ministry. Then a voice spoke from heaven and said, "This is my beloved Son, in whom I am well pleased." The seal of heaven was on His thirty years of obscurity at home.

Jesus of Nazareth lives today; He is Head of the church. He is able to fill His people with His glory and with His power in order that the faithfulness of His human life may be imparted to them by the Holy Ghost. He is able to restore the years that the cankerworm has eaten. Let none of us allow past failures to keep him from getting on his feet and stepping forward to do what he believes to be God's will. If some disheartened Christian is reading this book, somebody who feels that his past will prevent him from taking a responsibility in the army of God, I bid him, in my Master's Name, *he strong and of a good courage; neither be thou dismayed, for the Lord thy God is with thee whithersoever thou goest.*

The second qualification of leadership is *a distinct call:* "There shall not any man be able to stand before thee all the days of thy life: as I was with Moses, so I will be with thee: I will not fail thee, nor forsake thee. Be strong and of a good courage: for unto this people shalt thou divide for an inheritance the land, which I sware unto their fathers to give them" (Joshua 1:5–6). This is the second source of strength for spiritual leadership—a distinct call.

Joshua knew perfectly well that Canaan was infested by a thousand foes. He knew that every inch of advance would be contested by the enemy. But a man assured of the call of God is invincible. Certainly he is very conscious of his deficiencies; he is aware of all the walled cities in the land, and of the broad river that he has to cross before he gets there. He knows something of the ridicule and the criticism which are forever the portion of those who would dare to stand for God. But, looking away from all these to the revealed purpose of God, he gives himself utterly and completely to be a channel through which the Divine will may be worked out.

Therefore, in relation to any duties which you would undertake for God, I want to say very earnestly that the supreme question is, not "Are we qualified?" but "Are we called?" Are you grasping for position, or are you called of God? Answer that to the Lord, in His presence. Nothing is more important in your life than the answer to that question.

A minister in London went to see a friend of his, who said, "I hear you have had a revival at your church."

"Yes," the minister answered, "we have had a wonderful time."

"And how many additions to your church roll did you get?"

"Additions, brother! We have had some blessed subtractions!"

If any of you are seeking a position of power in your church, I hope that you will resign—or get right with God. We need men of God, men who have been broken by the Spirit of God, men who desire only the glory of God in our churches today.

I pray that God will raise up a mighty army of men, humbled, broken, who will step into position because they are sure that God has called them. If that comes about, the river will be in front of us, but, praise the Lord, we will go right through it. We will attack walled cities; God will make His mountains a way; the river will dry up, and the cities will fall down. All that the people of God have to do is to go forward with the Lord Jesus Christ.

I remind you of the Master Himself, who was so sure of His vocation. Where did He get His strength to go steadfastly to Jerusalem? From where did He receive power to go up Calvary's hill and to allow Himself to be crucified, in weakness, yet in mighty power? Notice: "I come not to do my own will, but the will of him that sent me." "I delight to do thy will, O God." "My meat is to do the will of him that sent me and to finish his work." Never for one minute, in all His life, did our precious Lord allow one rival claim to the will of God.

That is the secret of power. If there is something in your heart drawing you away from the path of God's choosing, decide today. Let nothing ever stand between you and the good, and the perfect, and the acceptable will of God. Have a sure calling.

The third source of power and strength for Christian leadership is the indwelling of the Word of God. Notice Joshua 1:8: "This book of the law shall not depart out of thy mouth; but thou shalt meditate therein day and night, that thou mayest observe to do according to all that is written therein: for then thou shalt make thy way prosperous, and then thou shalt have good success." Here was the assured presence of God made real in daily experience by the indwelling of the Word of God.

Through the Word of God the Spirit of God comes in fullness on your life, and occupies your heart. Here is the secret of all power in leadership: to be possessed by the Son of God, to be strengthened by His indwelling power, and to be filled by His Spirit. And here is the only way: "Thou shalt meditate therein day and night." There is no short cut to holiness.

I am telling you this from personal experience, and, I believe, as I get it from the Old Book, that if a man would be holy he has to go to God in prayer and meditate on the Word. If a man would walk with God, if a man would live a holy life, if a man would assume authority and hold it down, because God holds him down, he has to know what it is to pay the price of a closed door—sometimes even his family are on the other side—for no Christian leader is more effective in his leadership than when he is alone with God, on his knees.

I have no magic formula for your holiness; I have no hocus-pocus treatment to offer you; I have no short cut to spiritual power for any of you. All I can do is to say to you: Get back to your Bible; "meditate therein day and night," and go down before God on your face in prayer. For the greatest transactions of a man's experience are made, not in a church, but behind closed doors.

This is the way our Lord went. The Lord Jesus believed in the authority of His Bible, the Old Testament. He quoted it as the only real basis for the marriage tie; He quoted the story of Jonah to prove His resurrection. He used His Bible in temptation, and many times over, when confronted by the devil, He said, "It is written." Yes, His power came from steeping His life in the Word of God.

"The words that I speak unto you," says the Lord Jesus, "they are spirit and they are life." To be saturated with the Word of God is to be assured of the presence of God. Then, praise God, no weapon formed against us shall prosper. Every tongue raised against us in judgment He will condemn. Though the furnace be heated seven times hotter, He is with us, and though the river be broad and deep, He has promised that it shall never overflow us. "Fear not, for I am with thee." Then the weakling is made a conqueror, for God uses the weakling and the nobody to be a channel through whom He expresses His Will. That is the man God uses!

A faithful past, a sound vocation, a filling with the Word of God—what can we do to prove worthy of Him? Let us take our weakness, and our trembling, and our fears before Him; let there be an absolute submission to the indwelling power of His blessed Spirit. Let us ask that all these qualities that were revealed in Christ be imparted to us, that they may be real in your life and mine.

There is a price to be paid. Are you willing to pay it? Cancel every responsibility in your life other than what you believe to be God's will for you. Deliberately refuse any engagement which will keep you from meditation on His

Word. We are living in an age which has lost the art of being silent with an open Bible and waiting for God to speak.

Practice holiness, beginning today! If you are guilty of seeking position for position's sake, resign, or, alone with God, confess your sin and get right with Him. Then, through the church, through all its leadership, will be expressed heavenly light, heavenly authority, heavenly power, and the river of God will surely flow through each of us in great blessing to others.

# CHAPTER 3

# COUNTING THE COST

## JOSHUA 1:11

*And Joshua the son of Nun sent out of Shittim two men to spy secretly, saying, Go view the land, even Jericho. And they went, and came into an harlot's house, named Rahab, and lodged there.*

*And it was told the king of Jericho, saying, Behold, there came men in hither to night of the children of Israel to search out the country.*

*And the king of Jericho sent unto Rahab, saying, Bring forth the men that are come to thee, which are entered into thine house: for they be come to search out all the country.*

*And the woman took the two men, and hid them, and said thus, There came men unto me, but I wist not whence they were:*

*And it came to pass about the time of shutting of the gate, when it was dark, that the men went out: whither the men went I wot not: pursue after them quickly; for ye shall overtake them.*

*But she had brought them up to the roof of the house, and hid them with the stalks of flax, which she had laid in order upon the roof.*

*And the men pursued after them the way to Jordan unto*

*the fords: and as soon as they which pursued after them were gone out, they shut the gate.*

*And before they were laid down, she came up unto them upon the roof;*

*And she said unto the men, I know that the Lord hath given you the land, and that your terror is fallen upon us, and that all the inhabitants of the land faint because of you.*

*For we have heard how the Lord dried up the water of the Red sea for you, when ye came out of Egypt; and what ye did unto the two kings of the Amorites, that were on the other side Jordan, Sihon and Og, whom ye utterly destroyed.*

*And as soon as we had heard these things, our hearts did melt, neither did there remain any more courage in any man, because of you: for the Lord your God, he is God in heaven above, and in earth beneath.*

*Now therefore, I pray you, swear unto me by the Lord, since I have shewed you kindness, that ye will also shew kindness unto my father's house, and give me a true token:*

*And that ye will save alive my father, and my mother, and my brethren, and my sisters, and all that they have, and deliver our lives from death.*

*And the men answered her, Our life for yours, if ye utter not this our business. And it shall be, when the Lord hath given us the land, that we will deal kindly and truly with thee.*

*Then she let them down by a cord through the window: for her house was upon the town wall, and she dwelt upon the wall.*

*And she said unto them, Get you to the mountain, lest the pursuers meet you; and hide yourselves there three days, until the pursuers be returned: and afterward may ye go your way.*

*And the men said unto her, We will be blameless of this thine oath which thou hast made us swear.*

*Behold, when we come into the land, thou shalt bind this line of scarlet thread in the window which thou didst let us down by: and thou shalt bring thy father, and thy mother, and thy brethren, and all thy father's household, home unto thee.*

*And it shall be, that whosoever shall go out of the doors of thy house into the street, his blood shall be upon his head, and we will be guiltless: and whosoever shall be with thee in the house, his blood shall be on our head, if any hand be upon him.*

*And if thou utter this our business, then we will be quit of thine oath which thou hast made us to swear.*

*And she said, According unto your words, so be it. And she sent them away, and they departed: and she bound the scarlet line in the window.*

*And they went, and came unto the mountain, and abode there three days, until the pursuers were returned: and the pursuers sought them throughout all the way, but found them not.*

*So the two men returned, and descended from the mountain, and passed over, and came to Joshua the son of Nun, and told all things that befell them:*

*And they said unto Joshua, Truly the Lord hath delivered into our hands all the land; for even all the inhabitants of the country do faint because of us.*

JOSHUA 2:1–24

In our previous meditations on the book of Joshua we have come, I trust, to know and to realize that the Canaan of the Old Testament corresponds to the land of full blessing which awaits us all here and now in Jesus Christ our Lord. It is the purpose of God's redemption: He has brought us out that He might bring us in.

This land cannot be entered by moral effort or by moral attainment. It is entrusted by God to a representative, Joshua of the Old Testament, Jesus of the New, and through that representative the blessing is bestowed on God's people. It is to be possessed by faith: "Every place that the sole of your foot shall tread upon, that have I given unto you." So it is with us. God has blessed us with all spiritual blessings in Christ, but every blessing has to be claimed by faith and reckoned as ours through Jesus our Lord.

We come to a most significant point in the story, where the people of God were about to enter into the land of Canaan, and we discover that they had to wait for three days. "Then Joshua commanded the officers of the people, saying, Pass through the host, and command the people, saying, Prepare you victuals; for within three days ye shall pass over this Jordan, to go in to possess the land, which the Lord your God giveth you to possess it" (Joshua 1:10–11).

The hardest thing for any of us to do is to sit still and do nothing, to wait until we inherit the promises. But God has a great purpose to fulfill in every waiting time, although so often His people miss the purpose because of impatience with the Lord during the time of waiting. I want to think with you about that waiting time, the sitting still and counting the cost of what it means to inherit the blessing in Jesus our Lord.

Why were the people commanded to wait, and told that in three days they would pass over Jordan? We will observe three simple truths in this particular portion of scripture, and may the Holy Spirit write them on our hearts.

First, there was a soul to be saved. Joshua (the story is in the second chapter) sent two spies into the city of Jericho, and they came to Rahab's house.

Now, life in Jericho was proceeding as usual, business was in accordance with everyday custom; but the city was under the sentence of the judgment of God. The inhabitants boasted of the river that lay between them and the invading army on the other side. They were proud of their city, of its walls, and of its fortresses, but before heaven their iniquity was full. There was no question of making terms with the inhabitants of Jericho—within two weeks God would strike in judgment and the city would lie in a heap of ruins.

But within the city there was one life that had faith in God—not a very strong faith, not by any means a perfect faith, but Rahab believed in the living God, and was not ashamed to reveal that she did. Her faith was of such quality, at least, that we find reference to it in the picture gallery of the heroes of faith in Hebrews, chapter 11. It is also commented on by the Apostle James, who remarks that Rahab's faith—unlike the faith of some people—was evidenced by her works, and therefore she was justified in the sight of God. She had sufficient faith to identify herself with God's people, to put a scarlet thread outside her window.

Because of her faith, and the shelter she gave to God's people in her home, she became a sharer in all the blessings of the land of Canaan. She became part of the line of the ancestry of Jesus Christ Himself. This woman's faith produced works, and works brought down blessing.

There was a soul to be saved, and until that soul was saved the judgment of God was held back. That is always God's way in dealing with men. One righteous man lived in the city of Sodom, and God could do nothing to it until that man for whom He had purposed deliverance was out of the city. One feeble, sinful, immoral woman had but to touch the hem of the garment of Jesus, and His progress toward Calvary was arrested that He might save her soul. One poor, blind beggar cried from the roadside, "Oh, Jesus, have mercy upon me," and what all the people could not do, what the disciples could not do, because His face was set towards Jerusalem, the cry of a needy soul did—at his cry Jesus stood still. It has always been the way of the Master—He is not willing that one should perish.

We live in a world that is under the judgment of God, and there can be no question of the church coming to terms with it. We are told today by some people that we must catch the spirit of the age. God forbid! Our task is to rebuke the spirit of the age and challenge it for Jesus Christ. The world is under the judgment of God, but at the right hand of our Father in heaven is a Saviour whose blood speaks, and, until every ransomed soul for whom God in His sovereign grace has a purpose of salvation is delivered, the judgment is delayed.

How did Rahab get her faith? It was merely hearsay, for she had never met God personally. "She said unto the men [the spies], I know that the Lord hath given you the land, and that your terror is fallen upon us, and that all the inhabitants of the land faint because of you" (Joshua 2:9). This poor, sinful woman came to have faith in the reality of a living God because of the supernatural evidences that she saw in the life of God's people. All the people of the land had begun to faint because of the armies of God. The terror of the Lord gripped them. When they saw the invading army beginning to prepare to cross the river, they became conscious that, in spite of their walls and their defenses, they were helpless, because the invading army had God with it.

The most potent factor in the saving of a soul is the super-natural evidences of the presence of God in the life of a child of God. I challenge you in His name—what evidences of the supernatural are to be found in you and me? The evidences that God expects to find are not to be found in the correctness of our creed, but in the chastity of our character. And the evidences for which the world looks are not in what a Christian believes, but in how a Christian behaves. God looks for a man with a big heart, a man with a big love, a man with a great mercy in his dealing with others, a man whose charity and love take in all the people of God, a man who can be trusted with the confidence of anybody, because he is not only a loving man, but a righteous man.

There was a soul in Jericho to be saved, and that woman's faith resulted from the evidences of the supernatural she saw in the people of God.

Then, again, there was a separation to be confirmed. The closing verses of the first chapter of the book of Joshua give us the background. Joshua spoke during those three days, you will remember, to two and a half tribes of the people of God: the tribe of Reuben, Gad, and the half-tribe of Manasseh. The story of those two and a half tribes will be found in the book of Numbers, chapter 32.

In the course of the wilderness journey, the people of Reuben, Gad, and Manasseh came to a portion of land which was very fertile. They saw in it wonderful grazing lands and pasture for their flocks. It was a land, potentially, of great wealth. They were a rich people—they had many flocks and much cattle, and so they approached Moses and said, "We would rather stay here, on the east side of Jordan. This is all that anybody could desire. We don't want to go into Canaan.

We won't be bothered with all the trouble you are in for when you get over there. It will be easier for us here."

Moses agreed with their decision. He could do nothing else, for every man has a right to choose the level of life on which he himself is going to live. They were permitted to stay on the east side of Jordan and inherit this fertile bit of the wilderness on one condition—that before they inherited that land on the wilderness side of Canaan they must take their part in the battle to see the people of God into the land. Moreover, Moses gave them the privilege of leading the army. The tribes of Reuben and Gad and Manasseh were to go into Canaan first, and they were to start the march around Jericho in the leading position. Then, when they had tasted the fruit of the land and had the thrill of victory, Joshua would confirm their choice, that they still wanted to go back to the wilderness.

What a moment when Joshua now addresses the two and a half tribes, reminding them of their decision, and asking them what they were going to choose. You will observe that their choice was confirmed. They were perfectly willing to fulfill the bargain, to go into the land, lead the army and taste of the victories, but they were determined to go back to the comfort of the wilderness, the enjoyment and the indulgence of it. They said, "It is easier that way."

All His people, every ransomed soul, however weak or however strong his faith may be, God has sheltered in a crucified Lord. From before the foundation of the world, one whole and complete church, composed of the elect people of God, has been placed on redemption ground in Jesus Christ our Lord. God has taken hold of every man and woman for whom He has an eternal purpose of salvation, and lifted them, in Christ, into heavenly places. God has taken the weakest Christian, the Christian most conscious of failing, together with the pillar of the church, the strongest saint ever born, and has placed a whole, complete church in Jesus on resurrection ground. Neither the weakest Christian nor the strongest Christian struggles toward victory—he stands in it. Nor does either fight to achieve a blessing—he steps up by faith and accepts all that God has for him. In Jesus Christ, that is our position. If you are a believer in the Lord Jesus, however weak you are, however worldly or carnal you may be, however feeble your Christian faith is, I tell you that, in the sight of God, you are on redemption ground in Jesus Christ. That is our position.

But the question of where we spend our Christian experience, and on what level we live our Christian life, is left for us to choose. I may enjoy the blessing of Canaan for a while. I may enter into the land of full blessing. I may go with the people of God over this Jordan, up out of the wilderness. I may share some of the victories that are mine in Jesus, but I may yet be caught by sin, trapped by worldliness, beaten by compromise, and ensnared by the devil.

If a man is truly born again of the Spirit of God he will never be lost. I believe in the abiding security of the believer. Of course I do, provided he is a real believer, which means a man who has committed his life to Jesus Christ. But at any moment in my Christian life I can look into the face of the Lord Jesus and say to Him, "Lord, I have gone far enough now. I can't stand it—this conflict is too big, the war is too intense. Lord, I have gone far enough in my separation and in my Christian life."

*God has His best things for the few who dare to stand the test;*

*God has His second best for those who will not take His*
*best;*
*It is not always open ill that risks the promised rest;*
*The better often is the foe that keeps us from the best.*

Look through the terrifying record of the consequences
of that choice made by those two and a half tribes. Read I
Chronicles, chapter 5. You will discover that these tribes,
who had tasted of God's best and enjoyed God's victory,
who had led the army of the people of God into the land of
blessing, were the first to be captured by Assyrians when
they invaded Israel. Taken captive, they never returned.
They went down to defeat and into bondage, even though
at one time they had led the people of God in the way of
blessing. Judges 5:16 says this: "For the divisions of Reuben
there were great searchings of heart." I should think there
were! They chose, they tasted of blessing, they had entered
into the land of promise, but they hankered after the world,
its pleasures, its indulgence, and its sin, and they were
trapped and caught and ensnared in it.

It is not how a man begins his Christian life, but how he
ends it, that counts. It is one thing to come forward at a
meeting in answer to the appeal of an evangelist, with ten
thousand people looking on, or to hold your hand up, and to
sign a card. If it is real, the Lord bless you! But the thing
that matters is whether, following that decision, you press
into the land of blessing! Do you go on with God, do you
persistently, patiently, and in the face of every opposition
and every testing, go right through? And if you slip and fall
down, do you pick yourself up again and go on, or do you
go back into indulgence and sin?

I remember in childhood days, during the first World

War, on a certain lovely summer afternoon I was walking with my father along the pier at Tynemouth, near Newcastle, England. We noticed a crowd of people around and many ships in the harbor. Presently a cloud of smoke appeared in the distance, grew larger, and soon a convoy of battleships came into the river Tyne, and in the center of them there was one battleship heeling over—I wondered how it had remained afloat. It was H.M.S. *Lyon*, coming back from the battle of Jutland, a naval battle which turned the attack of Germany on our country at that time. As the ship got nearer the harbor, I saw great holes in her deck. She had no mast, no funnel, no turrets; the bridge had gone; the deck was just a shambles. Water was pouring in and out of her as she was being gently nursed home by tugs and an escort of ships. Shall I ever forget the sight of twenty-five sailors and one officer standing rigidly at attention on a part of the deck, with a tattered bit of the royal ensign flying from a piece of wreckage? Every throat that could cheer, cheered, and every ship that had a siren blew it. These twenty-six were all that were left, a tragic remnant of 1,100 men. But the ship had held on, she had fought through to the end, and she came into harbor victorious, holed and wounded, with hundreds of men killed—but still afloat and undaunted!

In the course of the Christian life we suffer many wounds from Satan, and sometimes from friends. If one day, however, when we get into the heavenly harbor, we get a welcome like that ship received, and hear the Lord Jesus say, "Well done, thou good and faithful servant, enter into the joy of thy Lord," we will care for nothing else, for it will have been worth it all when we see Jesus.

Now, one other thing about this waiting period, sanctification was to be completed. "Sanctify yourselves: for tomorrow the Lord will do wonders among you" (Joshua 3:5). The wonder-working power of God depends always on the sanctification of His people. A sovereign God so limits His sovereignty in speaking through His church to a world that is under judgment that He goes no further in saving the sinner than the saint is prepared to go in holiness before the Lord. The level on which God meets men depends on the level on which we as Christians are prepared to meet our Lord.

We all long to see God work wonders. Oh, how we have prayed that the fir tree might grow in our character instead of the thorn, that it might show gentleness instead of unkindness! How we have prayed in our home that instead of being like a desert it might blossom like the rose, and we appear before the Lord Jesus like a watered garden, full of fragrance!

How we have prayed for our churches, that God would give us another Pentecost and visit us in this mid-century with true revival! Why do we wait in vain? Why in your life is there still the thorn, and why in your home is there still the desert? Why in our churches is there still the bankruptcy of our modern experience? God does not wait for clever people; He wants clean people. Are we clean enough for God to use? Are we humble enough for God to entrust us with blessing, or would we take the glory to ourselves?

I know that we can be sanctified only by the God of peace. Yet though holiness, in the positive sense, is nothing more and nothing less than the indwelling and infilling of the Holy Ghost, expressing the life of the Lord Jesus in me, on the negative side it is the putting away of all known sin. Have we done that? Are we clean enough for God to give us revival? Are we broken enough and humble enough for

God to use us, or are we to go through our lives on the wretched wilderness level of failure and see nothing happen?

Let me go back for a moment to the first World War. In Flanders, you will remember, the battle of the Marne was a critical battle. General Foch was in a tight place. He had one thin line of troops between the Germans and Paris, and he knew that if Paris were lost, everything would be lost. He consulted his officers, heard their reports, and then announced, "My right is defeated, my left is broken—I attack!"

The challenge to the church today is identical with that in New Testament times. On the right is the Sadducee, bankrupt in his theology, the modernist who can explain away anything, whose foundations have crumbled around him since these two world wars—on the right, defeat.

On the left is the Pharisee, proud of his religion, proud of his law, proud of his theology, a fundamentalism which continually adds to the commandments of the law, and carefully dots all its i's and crosses all its t's. Refusing fellowship with anybody who does not agree with him, the Pharisee is as useless and helpless to meet world needs today as the liberal; from behind his fundamentalist barrier, he argues with his brother about this belief and that, and displays little love and charity—all in the name of a theoretical fundamentalism.

On the right, liberalism—bankrupt, beaten; on the left, fundamentalism—broken, baffled. In the name of heaven, let the army of God attack, for between the defeated liberals and the broken fundamentalists there is a center position. From the man in the fundamentalist camp let us take all his creed, and all his faith, all his beliefs in the Word of God. Let us not sacrifice one word of them, God helping us! From the man in the liberal camp let us learn from his love, his sincerity, and his open-heartedness. Let us take the best from both camps, and, in the name of the Lord Jesus, attack!

"Prepare you victuals; . . . ye shall pass over this Jordan to go in to possess the land, which the Lord your God giveth you to possess it (Joshua 1:11). Sanctify yourselves . . . for . . . the Lord will do wonders among you" (Joshua 3:5).

# CHAPTER 4

# THE ROYAL ROAD TO BLESSING

## JOSHUA 3:11

*And Joshua rose early in the morning; and they removed from Shittim, and came to Jordan, he and all the children of Israel, and lodged there before they passed over.*

*And it came to pass after three days, that the officers went through the host;*

*And they commanded the people, saying, When ye see the ark of the covenant of the Lord your God, and the priests and Levites bearing it, then ye shall remove from your place, and go after it.*

*Yet there shall be a space between you and it, about two thousand cubits by measure: come not near unto it, that ye may know the way by which ye must go: for ye have not passed this way heretofore.*

*And Joshua said unto the people, Sanctify yourselves: for to morrow the Lord will do wonders among you.*

*And Joshua spake unto the priests, saying, Take up the ark of the covenant, and pass over before the people. And they took up the ark of the covenant, and went before the people.*

*And the Lord said unto Joshua, This day will I begin to*

*magnify thee in the sight of all Israel, that they may know that, as I was with Moses, so I will be with thee.*

*And thou shalt command the priests that bear the ark of the covenant, saying, When ye are come to the brink of the water of Jordan, ye shall stand still in Jordan.*

*And Joshua said unto the children of Israel, Come hither, and hear the words of the Lord your God.*

*And Joshua said, Hereby ye shall know that the living God is among you, and that he will without fail drive out from before you the Canaanites, and the Hittites, and the Hivites, and the Perizzites, and the Girgashites, and the Amorites, and the Jebusites.*

*Behold, the ark of the covenant of the Lord of all the earth passeth over before you into Jordan.*

*Now therefore take you twelve men out of the tribes of Israel, out of every tribe a man.*

*And it shall come to pass, as soon as the soles of the feet of the priests that bear the ark of the Lord, the Lord of all the earth, shall rest in the waters of Jordan, that the waters of Jordan shall be cut off from the waters that come down from above; and they shall stand upon an heap.*

*And it came to pass, when the people removed from their tents, to pass over Jordan, and the priests bearing the ark of the covenant before the people;*

*And as they that bare the ark were come unto Jordan, and the feet of the priests that bare the ark were dipped in the brim of the water, (for Jordan overfloweth all his banks all the time of harvest,)*

*That the waters which came down from above stood and rose up upon an heap very far from the city Adam, that is beside Zaretan: and those that came down toward the sea of the plain, even the salt sea, failed, and were cut off: and the people passed over right against Jericho.*

*And the priests that bare the ark of the covenant of the Lord stood firm on dry ground in the midst of Jordan, and all the Israelites passed over on dry ground, until all the people were passed clean over Jordan.*

JOSHUA 3: 1–17

As we pursue our way through this wonderful Old Testament book of Joshua we come to that momentous event in the history of the children of Israel when they crossed from the wilderness into the land of Canaan. The crossing of Jordan does not illustrate the passing of a soul into eternity, but rather does it illustrate the passing of a Christian from one level of Christian life to another. It marks the end of the self-life and the beginning of the Christ-life: the end of a life lived on the principle of effort and the beginning of a life lived on the principle of faith and obedience. Between these two rolls the mighty river Jordan—a river of impossibility.

Are you intensely dissatisfied with the quality of Christian life you are living? Have these chapters opened up to you another possibility of life on a higher plane? But you have been tempted to close this book as you have said instinctively, "Not for me. That man just doesn't know my life. He doesn't know the impossibilities with which I have to cope."

No, my friend, I do not know your problems, but I know my Lord, with whom nothing is impossible. Therefore, if some of you face mountains of impossibility, and you say to yourself wistfully that life can never be any different for you, I believe that the Lord has something to say to you through His Word that can mark the end of your defeat by the impossible, and the beginning of a life of victory which overcomes the world, even your faith in God.

Therefore, let me ask you very carefully and attentively to follow me as we think of this great army of two and a half million people crossing over the river Jordan. For "Behold, the ark of the covenant of the Lord of all the earth passeth over before you into Jordan" (Joshua 3:11).

Verse 10 records, "Joshua said, Hereby ye shall know that the living God is among you, and that he will without fail drive out from before you the enemy." We see that the prospect which confronted the Israelites that day was one of conflict, but also of victory. The land of Canaan was inhabited by seven nations—all named for us in this verse. God commanded that every one of them should be exterminated.

I must pause for a moment here, for some of you may question the character of a God who could ever exterminate human life, and you may be tempted to say, "I could never believe in a God who would command that." Couldn't you? Four generations previously, God had promised to Abraham and to his seed this land for their possession. He said (Gen. 15:16), that in the fourth generation His people would come again to the land, for the iniquity of the Amorites within the land was not yet full.

Now, four generations later, the people of God were on the border of the land. The iniquity of the inhabitants was indeed full: they had been guilty of gross immorality, guilty of trafficking with evil spirits. In Deuteronomy 18:10, you remember, God warned His people that there could be no compromise with any soul which trafficked in spiritual evil; those who did so must be obliterated. Now the promise of God that He would drive them out from before His people is being fulfilled. The prospect which faced Israel was a conflict, not merely with men and women, please notice, but with the spiritual evil which was controlling the inhabitants of the land of Canaan.

This, of course, is a perfect analogy of the warfare of every child of God. "We wrestle not against flesh and blood, but against principalities, against powers, against the spiritual hosts of wickedness in heavenly places" (Eph. 6:11). The conflict which beset the children of Israel is of exactly the same character as the battle in which you and I are engaged every day of our lives. Do you realize that your personality is the field on which rages the battle between heaven and hell? On the one hand Satan and on the other hand God in Jesus Christ are battling to possess your life, the one that he may damage, the other that He may save. "We wrestle not with flesh and blood"—this was the nature of the conflict which faced the children of Israel in Canaan, and which faces us today.

But I would have you observe that they faced not only conflict but victory. God had a purpose for that land. What was it? This—a little babe in a manger at Bethlehem, Christ the Son of God on a cross at Calvary, one hundred and twenty people in an upper room and the Holy Ghost falling on them. Bethlehem, Calvary, Pentecost: the incarnation of the Son of God, the judgment of the sin of humanity heaped on Him, the life of the Son of God becoming incarnate in the believer; all this was God's master plan for the salvation of a fallen race. And nothing, I say *nothing*, on earth or in hell should ever stand in the way of the plan of God. The iniquity of the people was full. Now God begins to act.

God has a plan today for your life. What is it? Bethlehem, Calvary, Pentecost: the coming of the incarnate Jesus by the

Holy Spirit into your personality, the bearing of the judgment of your sins on the Cross and your death with Christ to all sin, the mighty power of the Third Person of the Trinity coming into a life that has consented to die with Christ. The purpose of God for every man and woman is Bethlehem, Calvary, Pentecost, and everything that stands in the way of God's fulfillment of His plan must be conquered.

But between that purpose and its realization flows Jordan, and it seems so impossible to cross it. In your mind, as I open up to you the purpose of God for your Christian experience, you are saying, "But what about the impossibility?" I wonder what it is. Is it the tyranny of habit? Could it possibly be that, in spite of your belief, you are mastered by passion? Could it be that you have never tasted deliverance from sin? Do you teach others, but have never been taught of God? Do you speak to others about the Lord Jesus, but have never known the conqueror in His power overcoming in your life? Maybe with you it is not some of these grosser things (though God knows it may be), but is it what we call the little things—the secret things, the hidden things—which to us seem not to matter, but which in the sight of heaven are equally appalling? With one it is an unloving spirit; with another it is a harsh judgment of other people. With yet others it is sensitiveness, feelings easily hurt, or proneness to stand up for themselves and their rights if their desires have been flouted, too great eagerness to vindicate themselves in any situation. Or maybe it is jealousy over the success of other people. It is these things, lurking deep down in Christian lives today, which mar the blessing and act as a barrier to revival. May God help us to see that these are the things in the Christian Church today which cripple our testimony, and that roll like a Jordan in flood between us and the land! The prospect is conflict and victory, but the experience hitherto has been conflict and defeat.

If you will take time to read this third chapter, you will find that everything centered around the Ark of the Covenant, the symbol of the presence of God. "Behold, the ark of the covenant of the Lord of all the earth passeth over before you into Jordan" (Joshua 3:11). No less than ten times in this chapter is there a direct reference to the Ark.

You will observe that, first of all, as the people crossed the Jordan, the Ark had to go in front of them. Every one of that two and a half million people had to have a clear, personal view of what happened to the Ark. Early in the morning the twelve priests took the Ark on their shoulders and marched toward the river, I can well imagine the feelings of that huge army as they witnessed the scene before them. Would it not be better to wait until the river had subsided and the flood season was over? Would it not be better to wait until they might be able to wade through when the river was low?

As the people watched, the twelve priests drew near to the river, but the flood still rolled by. They approached to within a yard of it, and still the river remained unchanged. But as they put their feet in the very edge of the water, the water began to roll back as if moved by a mighty hand, and the priests walked into the bed of the river on dry ground. Step by step, the water parted before them, and, as the Book states, "They stood firm . . . until all the people of God had passed clean over Jordan."

Likewise, neither can we get through to the Christ-life from the self-life unless each one of us has a clear, personal view of the Lord Jesus. That Ark went on in front, and whereas until then the whole army had been perplexed and in despair as they gazed at the impossible river, now their thoughts were centered on the fact that the Lord was with them, as symbolized by the Ark of the Covenant. As they saw the Ark go into the river, the waters parted, the river bed became dry, and the impossibility was overcome!

What has this to teach us? That Jesus the Saviour one day went into the garden of Gethsemane, where the flood rolled before Him. Then He went to a cross on the hill of Calvary, where it seemed as if the waters had submerged Him. He died, they laid Him in a tomb, outside of which was a sealed stone for a door. But that was not all: "Up from the grave He arose, with a mighty triumph o'er His foes." This Lord Jesus, writes Paul, "spoiled principalities and powers and made a show of them openly, triumphing over them" in his resurrection (Col. 2:15).

Do you begin now to see the way through? Our warfare is not against flesh and blood, but against principalities and powers. One day He, our High Priest, after the garden, the Cross, and the tomb, rose in triumph and spoiled our enemy. He repulsed every attack of Satan, and He rose, our victorious, conquering, coming King. Hallelujah! And to all that pass through the waters He said, "I will be with thee, and the river shall not overflow thee." The floods, the opposition of principalities and powers to the child of God, can never get past what our triumphant Lord Jesus conquered.

The passage of Jordan means facing the impossibility, following the dying, rising, ascending Jesus into the place of all power. Get a clear view of Him who can deal with the impossibility of your life before you have reached it. For in the name of the Lord Jesus I declare this truth, that, however subtle, however strong it may be, there is no attack of Satan on the child of God but first has struck the heart of the Lord. He overcame it at the Cross, and He bids us, His children, to get a clear view of Him, to face again the impossibility that we have faced so often, then look up into His face and say, "Now, Lord Jesus, I believe that, although I cannot, you can." In that moment the roar of Jordan will be silent, its violence be checked, and we will go through on dry land.

The path of the child of God from the wilderness to Canaan is by way of facing the impossible and looking up to a Risen Christ and getting hold of Him. "That's all very well," somebody says to me, "but isn't that all theory? How does the power of it come into my heart?"

"The priests that bare the ark of the covenant of the Lord stood firm on dry ground in the midst of Jordan, and all the Israelites passed over on dry ground, until all the people were passed clean over Jordan" (Joshua 3:17).

> Dear dying Lamb, Thy precious blood
> Shall never lose its power,
> Till all the ransomed Church of God
> Be saved to sin no more.

The power we need is in Jesus Christ henceforth: He holds back the fire of sin and temptation; He keeps back the impossible. The children of Israel approached and saw the desirable land in the distance, but realized that between them and it was this flooded river. They saw the blessing, but between them and the blessing was an impossibility. Does that describe you today? You see the possibility of blessing, you see life on a new level, you recognize that your life has been defeated and far from fulfilling God's intentions, but be-

tween the blessing and you there is Jordan. You must step by
faith up to the impossibility.

The people put their feet to the brink of the river and it
was dried up before them by the presence of the Ark of the
Covenant. They had been told to watch the Ark as they went
through, and, with their eyes away from the land of blessing
they saw only the Ark of the Covenant. Therefore, as they
went through the river, the Ark was between them and the
impossibility.

There is exposed all the difference between the wilderness
life of defeat and the life of victory in the land; between
some of us here and the desired blessing flows the river of impossibility. Does shame, human nature, temperament, or
pride stand between the land of blessing and the Christian
like this flooded Jordan? Let a child of God get his eyes on
the Lord Jesus and then look: between the impossibility and
himself there HE is. After that the child of God does not
talk about "getting the victory." It isn't the victory he
wants, it is the Victor. He does not speak about "striving for
a new blessing" and "seeking to enter a new experience."
His eyes are on the Lord Jesus and he puts the Lord Jesus between himself and the onslaught of the devil, and looks up
into His face, and there is victory.

That is the royal road to blessing. That is the life in which
there is no self-interest, no sensitiveness to injustice; the life
which isn't provoked, which isn't jealous; the life which isn't
seeking a blessing, but which wants only the Lord Jesus.
Will you tread that road with me, will you by faith stand on
the impossibility, the thing that has gripped you in defeat for
years—will you stand on it, look up to Jesus, and put Him
between you and it? Say to Him, "Lord Jesus, from this mo-

ment on we face the impossibility, we put our feet by faith on it and look up into Thy face, and pray that Thou wilt keep it back and stand firm while we cross over this river and enter the land of blessing. May it be no more self, but Christ."

# PART II

*Conquering the Enemy*

# Chapter 5

# THE CROSS AND THE CHRISTIAN
## JOSHUA 5:9

*And it came to pass, when all the people were clean passed over Jordan, that the Lord spake unto Joshua, saying,*

*Take you twelve men out of the people, out of every tribe a man,*

*And command ye them, saying, Take you hence out of the midst of Jordan, out of the place where the priests' feet stood firm, twelve stones, and ye shall carry them over with you, and leave them in the lodging place, where ye shall lodge this night.*

*Then Joshua called the twelve men, whom he had prepared of the children of Israel, out of every tribe a man:*

*And Joshua said unto them, Pass over before the ark of the Lord your God into the midst of Jordan, and take you up every man of you a stone upon his shoulder, according unto the number of the tribes of the children of Israel:*

*That this may be a sign among you, that when your children ask their fathers in time to come, saying, What mean ye by these stones?*

*Then ye shall answer them, That the waters of Jordan were cut off before the ark of the covenant of the Lord; when it passed over Jordan, the waters of Jordan were cut off: and these stones shall be for a memorial unto the children of Israel for ever.*

*And the children of Israel did so as Joshua commanded, and took up twelve stones out of the midst of Jordan, as the Lord spake unto Joshua, according to the number of the tribes of the children of Israel, and carried them over with them unto the place where they lodged, and laid them down there.*

*And Joshua set up twelve stones in the midst of Jordan, in the place where the feet of the priests which bare the ark of the covenant stood: and they are there unto this day.*

*For the priests which bare the ark stood in the midst of Jordan, until every thing was finished that the Lord commanded Joshua to speak unto the people, according to all that Moses commanded Joshua: and the people hasted and passed over.*

*And it came to pass, when all the people were clean passed over, that the ark of the Lord passed over, and the priests, in the presence of the people.*

*And the children of Reuben, and the children of Gad, and half the tribe of Manasseh, passed over armed before the children of Israel, as Moses spake unto them:*

*About forty thousand prepared for war passed over before the Lord unto battle, to the plains of Jericho.*

*On that day the Lord magnified Joshua in the sight of all Israel; and they feared him, as they feared Moses, all the days of his life.*

*And the Lord spake unto Joshua, saying,*

*Command the priests that bear the ark of the testimony, that they come up out of Jordan.*

*Joshua therefore commanded the priests, saying, Come ye up out of Jordan.*

*And it came to pass, when the priests that bare the ark of the covenant of the Lord were come up out of the midst of Jordan, and the soles of the priests' feet were lifted up unto the dry land, that the waters of Jordan returned unto their place, and flowed over all his banks, as they did before.*

*And the people came up out of Jordan on the tenth day of the first month, and encamped in Gilgal, in the east border of Jericho.*

*And those twelve stones, which they took out of Jordan, did Joshua pitch in Gilgal.*

*And he spake unto the children of Israel, saying, When your children shall ask their fathers in time to come, saying, What mean these stones?*

*Then ye shall let your children know, saying, Israel came over this Jordan on dry land.*

*For the Lord your God dried up the waters of Jordan from before you, until ye were passed over, as the Lord your God did to the Red sea, which he dried up from before us, until we were gone over:*

*That all the people of the earth might know the hand of the Lord, that it is mighty: that ye might fear the Lord your God for ever.*

JOSHUA 4: 1–24

We have been emphasizing the striking analogy between the book of Joshua in the Old Testament and the letter to the Ephesians in the New Testament. The way to victory, to the life that God intends His child to live, is pictured graphically and challengingly in this Old Testament book. It relates, in the first few chapters, how these people approached the river Jordan, and now, in chapter 4, we find them on the other side of the river. They have established, as it were, a bridgehead in the land of Canaan.

In front of them lies Jericho and hundreds of other places like it that have to be captured. War is about to begin, for blessings and battles always go together in the Christian life. The greater the blessing, the greater the battle with the powers of darkness, and only the Christian who presses right in to God will secure His best. But before they engage in war, before they rush in to attack Jericho, the Israelites have to learn some vital lessons while they wait at Gilgal. To wait to receive instructions from God is what every Christian finds to be the hardest thing in life to do.

Some of us, by the grace of God, may have established a bridgehead in the land of blessing, for by faith we have crossed over Jordan. In the enthusiasm of the moment we would start to rush into the attack and sweep everything before us. Now there is a tremendous war confronting us as we seek to establish ourselves in the land of blessing, and before God entrusts us with battles and victories there are some salutary lessons we must learn.

Gilgal became holy ground to the people of Israel. Throughout this whole book of Joshua you will find that Gilgal was the base of all their operations against the enemy. It was also a place to which Joshua frequently returned in the midst of his battles. After his victories, and also occasionally after his defeats, he found himself again and again going back to Gilgal.

Not only was it the base of operations and often the focal point for readjustment, but always the line of communication between the battle fronts, and Gilgal had to be kept clear. This was the place where they entered the land, their supply base, as it were. If the people of God were to conquer in the fight, there must always be a clear road between the battle front and base, between the land of blessing and Gilgal, and nothing ever must block the line of communication.

There are six essential lessons that the Christian has to learn at Gilgal. Two of these lessons, which we are going to learn in this chapter, are absolutely vital to every child of God if he is going to enter into the life of victory and deliverance. This is not *a* way of victory in Christian living, but *the* way of victory. There are no two ways in the Word of God. This is not the way of a fanatic or a crank, or a way that a few extreme and peculiar Christian people may take. I desire to show to you the only path of deliverance, the only road on which you may travel, child of God, if you would really experience the victory of the Cross in your life.

First of all, Gilgal was *a place of remembrance*. In the early verses of the fourth chapter, God commands Joshua to take twelve stones out of the bed of the river and to put them on the victory side of Jordan as a lasting memory of what had happened that day. Joshua took them from the place where the feet of the priests had stood firm in Jordan. Not only so, but we read in the ninth verse that he took twelve more stones and put them in the river bed. Except when the Jordan was in flood, they would be visible at all times of the year—there in the river bed where the feet of the priests had stood, and, please note, where the people had walked.

Whenever Joshua returned from his defeats, which were only occasional, and from his victories, which were plentiful, and, indeed, not only when Joshua returned there, but when future generations returned there, they would always ask, "What mean these stones?" And the answer that was to be given, in the tenth verse of this chapter, was simply this, that there the feet of the priests had stood firm "until everything was finished that the Lord commanded Joshua to speak unto the people."

"Now, what is all that about?" somebody says. "Very interesting history, but what on earth has it to do with me?"

A great deal, my friend. The best commentary on the Bible is the Bible itself, and if I may throw the floodlight of New Testament revelation on this Old Testament story, I am brought face to face with the central theme of the whole Bible: the death and the resurrection of Jesus Christ our Lord. There at Calvary Jesus died; there He stood firm until everything that God the Father had commanded God the Son to say to His people was finished. There He completed the perfect and final work of salvation for the human race. There, once and for all, the sin question was settled, and now there is no controversy between heaven and earth on the issue of sin as we understand the term, for the issue today is a rejected, crucified, despised Redeemer. Man's sins, however gross they may be, or however mild they may be; however foul they may be, or however respectable they may be, were settled once and for all at Calvary.

But there is something more than that: not only did the priests go down into the bed of the river, you will observe, but the people went down too. The deepest, most real, and most wonderful meaning of Calvary is that not only did Jesus die there for my sins, but I died with Him and in Him. Without a real spiritual revelation to your heart of this, you will never be a victorious Christian.

Listen to the language of the Apostle Paul: "I am crucified with Christ: nevertheless I live; yet not I, but Christ liveth in me" (Gal. 2:20); "One died for all, then were all dead" (II Cor. 5:14); "Buried with him by baptism . . . that like as Christ was raised up . . . even so we also should walk in newness of life" (Rom. 6:4). The whole basis of operation, the supply base for Christian victory is the understanding—at least if not with your mind, then with your heart, and your acceptance of the fact by faith—that Jesus was not alone on the Cross, but that all His people went into death with Him.

A few years ago at Keswick, in England, at one of our great yearly missionary meetings, a missionary returned from China was giving her testimony. She said that before she went out to the mission field a friend of hers said to her, "What on earth are you going to bury yourself in China for? You'll never stand the climate—you'll be dead in six months." Cheerful advice to give a missionary!

But the missionary turned to her friend and said, "My dear girl, I want you to know that five years ago I died. When Jesus called me to China, I bowed my head at the Cross and died to everything except God and China." And I happen to know that this girl died to the possibility of a husband, a home, children, to her family, comforts, pleasure, luxury, all of which were within her grasp.

That, in the sight of God and the angels in heaven, is the only sane, real meaning of the Cross. There is no other way for any of us. When God speaks to us in Jesus, when God reveals His Son hanging there on the tree, He asks us to assent in our minds and in our hearts to the truth that we died with Him.

Now, I imagine that many of you have visions of some great project that you are going to do for God, but you are always planning a scheme and thinking out a method by which you can win souls to Jesus. Very good, but it is only second best. God's best for you is to die! For God has nothing else whatsoever for the most refined, educated, business man or woman, or, on the other hand, for the most profligate sinner. He has nothing for any of us, outside of Christ, except judgment and death; it must be "Jesus only"! The thing that God is calling on some people to do, people who want to do big things for Him, is to die with Jesus.

What does the Cross mean to you? It would be well to pause and to ask ourselves that question. Before God raises His people to victory, to the glory of His kingdom, He takes them down, down to the bedrock depths of Jordan. He asks them to be willing to die, for, said the Saviour, "Except a corn of wheat fall into the ground and die, it abideth alone: but if it die, it bringeth forth much fruit" (John 12:24).

Let the Holy Spirit apply this question to your heart: "Have you died with Christ?" Have you died to your reputation? To your point of view? To your self-esteem? Died even to some of the precious normal, natural things of life, but which are not God's will for you? Are you facing life's future with an ambition to serve God? Is it going to be the mission field, or is it going to be your boy friend, your girl friend, who hasn't been called to the place to which God has called you?

> O Cross that liftest up my head,
>    I dare not ask to fly from thee.
> I lay in dust life's glory, dead,
> And from the ground there blossoms red
>    Life that shall endless be.

Have I died? Gilgal is a place of remembrance.

But, thank heaven, our picture here is not only the negative but the positive—Gilgal is *the place of resurrection.*

"And the people came up out of Jordan on the tenth day of the first month," says verse 19 of chapter 4, "and encamped at Gilgal." On the tenth day of the first month, exactly forty years previously, they had marched out of Egypt. The passover lamb had been killed, the blood had been sprinkled, and the people had been delivered from the bondage of Egypt. But for forty years they had wandered in a wilderness of carnality, unbelief, and disobedience. Now they had come through Jordan and were encamped at Gilgal.

Do you know what that word "Gilgal" means? It means that "the reproach has been rolled away." I want to say here that any believer, man or woman, boy or girl, living in the wilderness of carnality and spiritual defeat and failure, is a reproach. But if we have established a bridgehead, and have crossed over Jordan, the reproach has been rolled away, and Gilgal is the place of resurrection.

"They came out of Jordan on the tenth day of the first month," and they all came out, although it might be that, years later, some might choose to go back into the wilderness. Let me remind you that though a man truly regenerate by the Spirit of God can never be lost, yet a man who presses into the land of blessing and steps into the place of victory can lose it and go back into the wilderness, and can end his life on the very verge of Egypt once more. That is why the Apostle Paul said, "I keep my body in subjection, I buffet it, I bruise it, I batter it, lest, having preached to others, I myself might be a castaway" (I Cor. 9:27). Do not imagine that a man can get a second blessing which puts him into a finality of grace. He may get into the land of blessing, but the next day go back into the wilderness. He may get into victory, but the next day be in the bondage of failure if he is not a man who observes this rule: Gilgal is the place of resurrection.

That is interesting history, but what does it mean to you and me? Just this: "Even when we were dead in sins, God hath quickened us together with Christ (by grace we are saved) and hath raised us up together, and made us to sit together in heavenly places in Christ Jesus" (Eph. 2:5, 6). That just thrills my soul! Do you see the meaning of it?

If you have never tasted victory, if you have never really entered into the liberty with which Christ has set us free, you will find the basis of all teaching concerning deliverance from sin just here. We are not only identified with Jesus in His death, but we are one with Him in His resurrection, and we are one with Him in His ascension. We all died with Him, we all went down into the grave with Him, we all rose with Him that first Easter morning, we ascended with Him into heavenly places, and we are there today, far above all principalities and powers.

But you may say, "I am sitting here, never feeling more with my feet on the earth than right now. What do you mean, that I am floating around in heavenly places with wings and harps?" I didn't say that, but you may have thought I was implying it.

May I explain? "We wait," says the Apostle Paul, "for the redemption of our bodies" (Rom. 8:23). We wait for it; we live here in the flesh, in a body which is under the stroke and effect of man's original fall into sin. So long as we are in this world we will be very conscious that we inhabit a body of corruption and death. We are constantly with it, and we know its nature, together with its appetites and its desires.

When Christ died, the self-life died, and He took a new life up to the throne of God when He ascended into heaven, and He poured out into the hearts of believers a life that is far above principality and power, a life that is seated with Him in heavenly places. In the flesh I am on the earth, but in the spirit I am in heaven. In the flesh I am subject to the devil. In the spirit I am with my Lord in glory.

Which is going to control my life, my body or my spirit? Which is going to decide my Christian career, this flesh of mortality and failure, or the spirit of liberty that Jesus has put within me? Am I going through my Christian life bound as a victim to this body of sin and temptation and lust? Or by faith am I going to take my place where I am in spirit with the Lord Jesus and say to the devil, "Get out. I'll have no part with you"?

I think of young boys and girls going into the ministry and going to be workers for the Lord, and grappling with this thing. Do you see a new possibility, do you understand that either you are going to let yourself be victimized by the flesh, or you are going to let yourself be conquered by the Holy Ghost?

It may seem like a dream, but it is faith that makes it real, and the only thing that Satan can do is to put doubts in your mind and tell you the thing is not true, when God's Word says it is true. Any Christian who, by faith, takes his position on victory ground is invincible. He who steps in by faith and claims that life which is far above all principality and power is beyond and out of the reach of the devil. Gilgal is the place of resurrection.

If any Israelite had gone back over Jordan into the wilderness, the stones in the bed of that river would have cried out against him. The stones that rested on the river bank would have cried out in protest that a people united in redemption and placed together on victory ground should go back to the wilderness. Do your standards of Christian life, your worldliness and compromise and sinfulness, cause the empty tomb of the Lord Jesus to cry out in protest? Get onto the victory side again: you have been placed there!

Gilgal is a place of resurrection, *but* it is resurrection only in the measure in which it is remembrance. It is life only in the measure in which it is death. It is victory only in the measure in which I have been humbled. It is triumph only in the measure in which I have gone down with the Lord Jesus to the grave.

# CHAPTER 6

# PREPARING FOR THE BATTLE

### JOSHUA 5:10

*And it came to pass, when all the kings of the Amorites which were on the side of Jordan westward, and all the kings of the Canaanites, which were by the sea, heard that the Lord had dried up the waters of Jordan from before the children of Israel, until we were passed over, that their heart melted, neither was there spirit in them any more, because of the children of Israel.*

*At that time the Lord said unto Joshua, Make thee sharp knives, and circumcise again the children of Israel the second time.*

*And Joshua made him sharp knives, and circumcised the children of Israel at the hill of the foreskins.*

*And this is the cause why Joshua did circumcise: All the people that came out of Egypt, that were males, even all the men of war, died in the wilderness by the way, after they came out of Egypt.*

*Now all the people that came out were circumcised: but all the people that were born in the wilderness by the way as they came forth out of Egypt, them they had not circumcised.*

*For the children of Israel walked forty years in the wilderness, till all the people that were men of war, which came out of Egypt, were consumed, because they obeyed not the voice of the Lord: unto whom the Lord sware that he would not show them the land, which the Lord sware unto their fathers that he would give us, a land that floweth with milk and honey.*

*And their children, whom he raised up in their stead, them Joshua circumcised: for they were uncircumcised, because they had not circumcised them by the way.*

*And it came to pass, when they had done circumcising all the people, that they abode in their places in the camp, till they were whole.*

*And the Lord said unto Joshua, This day have I rolled away the reproach of Egypt from off you. Wherefore the name of the place is called Gilgal unto this day.*

*And the children of Israel encamped in Gilgal, and kept the passover on the fourteenth day of the month at even in the plains of Jericho.*

JOSHUA 5: 1—10

If you were to glance at the opening verses of Joshua 5 you would see that a most interesting situation has developed in the career of the children of Israel. They have crossed from the wilderness into the land, and now terror has gripped the hearts of the enemy. Evidences of supernatural power at the disposal of God's people have caused panic in the camp of the foe.

I must not digress, but I would point out that any real evidence of the supernatural is the one thing above all else that is lacking in the witness of the Church of Christ today. The people of God (in this time of which we are thinking) bore such unmistakable proofs that the living God was with them, and had brought them miraculously out of the wilderness into the land of blessing, that their enemies were panic-stricken.

This was a strategic moment. Certainly it must be the right moment to launch an all-out offensive. But no, God is never in a hurry. God's delays are always infinitely more profitable than our haste. We are always in a fever to do something for God and have forgotten that the first thing God wants is that we should *be* something for Him. In this time of delay God had lessons to teach His people which were going to decide all the future course of warfare in the land.

In the last chapter I dealt with two of the six lessons, and we saw that Gilgal was a place of remembrance and a place of resurrection. I cannot possibly deal with four here, so we will have another two and leave the last two for the next chapter. Don't be impatient. Don't be so eager to rush ahead and tackle Jericho until we have learned the lessons at Gilgal that God would have us learn.

I believe that the whole future course, character, and testimony of the Church of Christ depends, not partly, but entirely, on the Spirit of God writing deeply in our hearts the lessons of His Word. I can but proclaim them; I am dependent entirely on the Spirit of God to convict your heart and conscience and make this truth be to you something real and dynamic in your experience.

We have therefore seen that Gilgal was a place of remembrance and a place of resurrection, a place where the people went down into Jordan and rose up on to resurrection ground, a place where the whole army of God came through from the wilderness into the land of Canaan, between which and the wilderness rolled the river Jordan. They were all now in the land of promise.

Also we saw that, in the New Testament sense of the

word, Gilgal speaks of the fact that the whole Church of Christ has been brought through Calvary, through death, on to resurrection ground, and that every child of God, no matter how weak, is in a position, potentially, of complete and absolute victory in the Lord Jesus. Between the Christian and the world stands the Cross. Between the Christian and sin lies Calvary, and any child of God redeemed by the blood and brought into the land of blessing who would seek to go back into the wilderness (and, indeed, he may) has to trample the Cross under foot and count the blood of the Covenant an unworthy thing.

Now, I want you to get hold of two more very wonderful things about Gilgal, very precious and very searching truths. First of all, is this: Gilgal was *the place of renunciation.* You will discover at the beginning of Joshua, chapter 5, that the rite of circumcision which had been in abeyance for the forty years of that wilderness journey was once again put into operation, and God commanded Joshua that the people should be circumcised. To understand what that means, look at Genesis 17: 10–14, and you will find that circumcision was the seal of God's covenant with Abram. It was the mark of the promise that Abram and his seed would possess the land of Canaan.

The rite of circumcision was an outward testimony to the fact that the land was to be possessed in the weakness of the flesh, through the suffering, very often, of the body. It symbolized the weakness and almost death, as it were, of everything that man can be, in order that the possession of the land should be given to them unmistakably in the sovereign grace of God. This had been suspended for nearly forty years in the wilderness because the people had been unbelieving and disobedient, but now they are brought into the land, and

the first thing that happened to them when they gained re
demption ground was that they were to submit to this pain
ful and humbling rite of circumcision.

Of course, it may seem strange that after we have the
people right on redemption ground, it looks now as if we
were taking them down and back again to the Cross, to
death and humiliation. But that is exactly Christian experience. The New Testament speaks of "the circumcision
which is not made with hands." Look at the language of Paul
in writing to the Colossians (2:10, 11): "And ye," says Paul,
"are complete in him, which is the head of all principality
and power: in whom also ye are circumcised with the circumcision made without hands, in putting off the body of
the sins of the flesh by the circumcision of Christ."

We need to understand that we are complete in Him; we
are all on redemption ground. All that we need is "in Jesus."
He has blessed us with all spiritual blessings in heavenly
places, and the whole Church of Christ, from the weakest to
the strongest, is on the victory side of the Cross.

That is the positive, but for every positive there is a negative. While every one of us has been collectively put in the
land of blessing and the place of victory, one by one each of
us has to step into the audience chamber of the King of
kings and there, with absolute honesty and complete trans-
parency, submit to the knife of the great Physician of souls.
It is something that we cannot do collectively; every one of
us has to do it alone, for himself: step into the Physician's
presence and surrender heart and will to Him, gaze on Calvary, and allow the Cross of Christ to be impressed on every
part of his personality.

Now, of course you may not see the reason for that. It
is this, in the language of Paul (and whose language could

I borrow with greater effect?): "For I through the law am dead to the law, that I might live unto God" (Gal. 2:19). What does he mean? Just this: through the perfect fulfilment of the law by my substitute, Jesus Christ, through His absolute obedience to the will of God, through His complete satisfaction of every requirement of God, I am dead to the law. In other words, the law, with its condemnation, has no further hold on me.

I was converted in a little public house in England called "The Grey Bull" when somebody showed me a Bible (I had not read it much before) and opened it for me at Romans 8:1: "There is therefore now no condemnation to them that are in Christ Jesus."

What a precious verse that was to me then! It does not say that if I try to be a good man and attend church every Sunday and say my prayers and read by Bible, I might be saved some day. It says, "There is therefore *now* no condemnation." I underlined that little word *now* so heavily that I went right through to the middle of Philippians and ruined my Bible on the first day. But it was worth the cost! "I through the law am dead to the law." It has no claim on me. All its demands have been settled and all its condemnation finished with in the person of Jesus Christ.

Now, that is true in position, but it also needs to be made true in personal experience, and that is something between myself and God. Every child of God comes to a point in his life when the Lord tests the reality of his acceptance of the position which God has offered him in Jesus Christ. That does not mean to say, of course, that I have to take every sin of which I am ever guilty and crucify them one by one. I could never do that; I would be at the business all day and all the years until I die and even then not be finished. It does not mean that I have to take this sinful flesh of mine and nail it to the Cross. But it does mean this: that I am to believe that Jesus has done it all for me. I am to believe that He has not left one sin or one habit or one failure of my life undealt with. I am to believe that in Jesus Christ all my sins and all my failures have been disposed of once and for all. I am to believe that, and then I am to give the consent of my will and of my heart to the Spirit of the living God indwelling my personality to make this transaction real.

Fellow Christian, this is, indeed, the most vital thing about your Christian walk and Christian character. It is only the Spirit of Christ who knows enough about you and about Satanic power, and who is therefore strong enough to deal with this situation in your heart. It is only Jesus who can bind the sacrifice of your life to the altar of Calvary. Only He in you can keep the flesh in the place of death. Only He sees enough, and only He knows enough, and only He is strong enough, to face it all. Only the Spirit of God can apply the withering fire of the Cross to keep dead the flesh, with its lusts, its ambitions, and its desires.

If anybody says that a Christian is a man from whose life the possibility of sin has been eradicated I cannot agree with him, nor do I believe that such a doctrine is to be found anywhere in God's Word. No, the possibility of sin is with us; we live in the body of sin, and we will be with it until we die. But also within us is a mightier power: the Spirit of Christ Himself, overcoming the power of the flesh. Therefore God asks me His child, and each one of us, to step into the audience chamber of the King of kings and yield to the knife for the pruning. "Every branch that beareth fruit, he purgeth it," says the Lord Jesus, "that it may bring forth more fruit" (John 15:2).

Is God withholding blessing from your Christian work? Is God not giving you any conversions? You are teaching a Sunday-school class of youngsters or grown-ups, a Bible class, or you are witnessing, or trying to, day by day, but you never see anything happen! What is your reaction to that? Do you say to yourself, "Well, of course God is sovereign, and I must leave the results to Him"? Do you make the sovereignty of God an excuse for your own sinful life?

Have you been led to assume that the fellowship of a Christian church consists of a minister and some colleagues and a little group of people in the "inner circle" who do the job, with everybody else a kind of spectator? Have you assumed that Christian responsibility is merely that? Have you not understood that God has redeemed you with the blood of Jesus Christ in order that through you He might reach another?

> God has no hands but your hands
>   To do His work today;
> He has no feet but your feet
>   To lead men in His way.

Maybe someone reading this has been a Christian for years and years and yet never has sat down beside one individual and led him to Christ. If that is true, there is something wrong somewhere, and it may be that you have refused to accept the application of the Cross of Christ to every part of your life. In position you are on redemption ground with every fellow believer. You are in the land, but in experience you are in the wilderness. I would bid you stay in Gilgal a while and encamp there and dig your roots deeply there, and consent to all the purpose of God for your life in Jesus Christ.

Have you refused to submit to the chastening of the Lord? Perhaps your body is racked with pain and you have fought against God's treatment of you. It may be that you have rebelled against His will, and you carry deep down in your soul a personal problem about which nobody else knows anything. Is it that deep down in your heart there are issues that your nearest and dearest friends can know nothing about, but which God knows as signs of rebellion?

Is it, perhaps, that God has spoken to you about His service in some other land and called you to some missionary enterprise, but you know perfectly well that to do so involves giving up some cherished loved one? You have stood in the presence of the Lord week by week, and you have met with His people, and God has spoken to you and revealed His purpose to you. He has been ready to take the knife and go deep into your heart, but you have said, "No!" Is that it?

Fellow Christian, do not be afraid of the knife. It is in the hand of the lover of your soul, Jesus your Saviour. Whatever be the cost, let Gilgal be for you today the place of absolute renunciation of everything that the Spirit of God reveals to you that is contrary to His will. That is Christian experience which is not merely the teaching of a doctrine but the living of a life. It is not merely the understanding of truth, it is looking into the face of Jesus and asking Him to make Calvary real in your soul, no matter what it may cost you. Do you dare face that renunciation?

But I am so glad to have another side of the picture to give you in this chapter, a positive side that is so wonderful it just thrills my soul to think about it! For not only did the people of God encamp at Gilgal, says Joshua 5:10, they "kept the passover on the fourteenth day of the month at even in the plains of Jericho." Gilgal was also *the place of restoration*.

The Passover had been observed only twice before: once, when the Israelites went out of Egypt and the other time at Mount Sinai. Since then there had been no Passover. This feast of worship, remembrance, and fellowship had been abandoned altogether. It had not been abandoned by choice but by God's command. He had commanded that no uncircumcised person should ever partake of the feast of the Passover (Exodus 12:48). They were not allowed to enjoy its feasting and the remembrance of God's victory on that Passover night. They had forfeited their right to it and surrendered their privileges by living in disobedience and unbelief. Because of that there was no Passover.

Let me say to you with all the earnestness of my heart that there can never be any feasting on the Lord in your heart, any real heart worship of God, if there is disobedience to God in your life. If sometimes Sunday worship means little to you, and sometimes you never get anything out of your Bible, ask yourself if this is not because you have forfeited your right to blessing. God is not going to give the enjoyment of His fellowship and His blessing to people who are content to live in disobedience. How often I hear it said of a church, "The place is absolutely dead!" I wonder if it is because the people are absolutely disobedient to the Word of God.

But immediately the rite of circumcision was renewed they kept the Passover. The moment they obeyed, heaven opened and they feasted in fellowship with God. At the moment that they were willing and submitted to the principle of death, at that moment God was real.

My heart goes out to him who has been in controversy with the Lord week after week, who has not absolutely surrendered to God. Beloved, the Lord is at your hand, waiting to bless you. The Lord is at your side, waiting to make Himself real to you if only you will give in. Immediately the rite of circumcision—at that moment, the Passover.

Of course, the shedding of the blood of the Lamb took place only once and the people came out of Egypt only once, but the feast was to be perpetuated in remembrance of that day. Centuries later it gave way to something even more wonderful when the Lord Jesus gathered a few disciples around Him and broke bread in the upper room in a ceremony that was to be a perpetual reminder of His death.

In years to come even that will pass away, when faith turns to sight and the people of God meet together around His table at the marriage supper of the Lamb of God. Five minutes in heaven will make up for a lifetime of agony and suffering, of conflict and battle to do the will of God. But until that day this is the purpose of God: that we should feast on our Lord Jesus.

You cannot do the work of heaven unless daily you eat the bread of heaven. You cannot speak for Jesus out of your lips unless, first of all, you are enjoying Him in your heart. The enjoyment of an indwelling Lord is an absolute essential to the proclaiming a living Christ with your mouth. How can you bring another soul to life if you yourself are nine-tenths dead spiritually? It is utterly and completely impossible. I know you can use your lips and give a Bible study; you can talk to a friend and quote texts; you can use sound and evangelical language, but as the years go by it literally has no effect.

You know why it is—you live at such a speed that you

never pause to enjoy Christ in your heart. If you were to sum up, not what you would like to tell other people, but what you know to be the truth, how much time have you spent in your own room with God during the past week? How much time have you actually been with God in the inner sanctum with an open Bible, and waited on Him? There your weakness could have absorbed His strength, and your restlessness and feverishness have been stilled by His power and peace, and your impatience have taken in the grace and long-suffering of the Lord Jesus Christ. Has that happened to you?

Listen to the language of this hymn:

> Drop Thy still dews of quietness
>   Till all our strivings cease;
> Take from our souls the strain and stress,
> And let our ordered lives confess
>   The beauty of Thy peace.
>
> Breathe through the heats of our desire
>   Thy coolness and Thy balm;
> Let sense be dumb, let flesh retire,
> Speak through the earthquake, wind, and fire,
>   O still, small voice of calm!

And we haven't given Him five minutes to do it!

Gilgal was a place of renunciation and a place of restoration, and it could be that to you just now. They encamped in Gilgal on the fourteenth day of the first month—how immediate the keeping of the Passover, four days after they crossed the river! And they kept it in the plains of Jericho! That thrills me—right under the nose of the devil! That is the place where we can just slip in and take the blessing of God. That is the place where we can defeat Satan; right in the teeth of his most subtle attacks we can have the victory from our heavenly Father!

There is no such thing in the Christian life as retiring into a monastery or a convent and there hoping that God will meet you and bless you. True, there are moments, as I have already said, when we need to get alone with God. But I have always found the blessedness of the truth that "he prepares a table before me in the presence of mine enemies." Feast on Christ in the thick of the fight, under the very nose of the devil, and prove to him that Jesus is Conqueror. That is Gilgal.

There is a place of restoration for you when there has been renunciation. Jesus waits to draw near to your heart now. Yet, because of some silly, stupid little idol that you keep on the throne of your heart, you may be forfeiting the right to His presence and to His power. Would you be willing at this moment for absolute renunciation, for the knife in the hand of the Husbandman to cut away the last vestige of decay?

If we are honest and mean business about it—immediately, the Passover. "When the burnt offering began, the song of the Lord began also" (II Chron. 29:27). When the child of God comes to the Master and is absolutely real in the presence of the Lord and consents to all the implications of the Cross, no matter what it may cost him, at that moment heaven opens, the joy of the Lord floods his soul, and the peace that passes all understanding fills his heart—and it is taking place in the very presence of his enemies!

# CHAPTER 7

# THE REWARD OF REALITY

JOSHUA 5:12

*And the children of Israel encamped in Gilgal, and kept the passover on the fourteenth day of the month at even in the plains of Jericho.*

*And they did eat of the old corn of the land on the morrow after the passover, unleavened cakes, and parched corn in the selfsame day.*

*And the manna ceased on the morrow after they had eaten of the old corn of the land; neither had the children of Israel manna any more; but they did eat of the fruit of the land of Canaan that year.*

*And it came to pass, when Joshua was by Jericho, that he lifted up his eyes and looked, and, behold, there stood a man over against him with his sword drawn in his hand: and Joshua went unto him, and said unto him, Art thou for us, or for our adversaries?*

*And he said, Nay; but as captain of the host of the Lord am I now come. And Joshua fell on his face to the earth, and did worship, and said unto him, What saith my lord unto his servant?*

*And the captain of the Lord's host said unto Joshua, Loose*

*thy shoe from off thy foot; for the place whereon thou
standest is holy. And Joshua did so.*

JOSHUA 5:10–15

In the preceding two chapters we paused with the children
of Israel on the banks of Jordan while we sought with them
to prepare ourselves for the spiritual battles confronting us.

Gilgal, as I have already said, became a key place for
them. It has, I believe, been a testing place for some of us.
We have had to learn lessons there which have not been easy
to learn. But we have come to understand that before there
can be a Pentecost there must be a Calvary, and before there
can be the outpouring of the rivers of living water from the
throne of God through the hearts of His people there must be
death to ourselves and the absolute abandonment to God's
will for us.

I rather imagine that some of you may have been saying,
"Is it worth it? Need I pay such a big price? Surely I can
afford to be less ruthless with myself and less real with God.
Do I need to go so far? Surely it is possible to get away with
life on a Christian level that does not demand so much of me
personally."

Of course, the answer to that question is, "Yes, it is perfectly possible." Indeed, the fact that so many people are
content with a second-best experience is patently evident
today. That is the reason why the Church of God in this tremendous hour is so incapable of matching the situation with
heavenly resources and heavenly authority.

Only a man filled with the Spirit of God, who is on fire for
God and who is living in New Testament experience of a
holy life, can ever match the challenge of this age. The mil
lions of people committed one hundred per cent to Com

munism can be resisted and overcome, I believe, by a comparatively small handful of Christian people who are committed to the same degree to the cause of Christ.

But where are they? The tragedy is that too often those who think they are sound in doctrine, and who think they have the answer from the Word of God, are lacking in devotion to our Lord. Too often those who think they know something of their Bible and understand what God is doing in the world, who recognize that the days are short and soon Jesus our Lord will be here again and it will be too late then—too often, I say, such people are occupied with trying to make the machinery of the church work. Too often they are occupied in trying to settle personal differences and to get along with each other. Too often the whole machinery lacks the oil of the Spirit of God. It is a tragic thing that men right in doctrine, right in head, are so often wrong in heart. Oh that we might see the irony of this picture and face again the need for being one hundred per cent committed to the Lord Jesus Christ before it is too late!

There are two further lessons that we must learn at Gilgal before we can start a warfare against the enemy. We have learned thus far that Gilgal was a place of remembrance and resurrection. It was also a place of renunciation and of restoration, where fellowship with God was renewed. Now I want to show you from these verses in Joshua that it is yet further a place of realization and of revelation. "And the manna ceased on the morrow after they had eaten of the old corn of the land; neither had the children of Israel manna any more; but they did eat of the fruit of the land of Canaan that year" (Joshua 5:12).

You will observe that there are three successive days mentioned in this portion of God's Word. On the fourteenth day they kept the Passover; the very next day they ate of the corn of the land, and the day after that the manna ceased. How quickly God responds to obedient children! How swiftly do the forces of heaven operate when the people of God get right with Him!

On that very same day of the year that they began to take of the fruit of the land, centuries later Jesus Christ our Lord rose from the tomb. Does not this picture the moment in Christian experience when we first begin to realize that all our resources are to be drawn from a risen, victorious Lord?

When a Christian begins to count upon His presence, to reckon upon His victory, and to draw upon His power, it is like stepping into a totally different world! The child of God finds that his faith which has been firmly rooted at the Cross now starts to bear fruit because he is in living touch with the throne of God. Isn't it a new stage in Christian experience when we look not only back to Calvary but also up to a living Christ on the throne? We begin to draw infinite, heavenly power every moment of every day from Him, and we discover that the Christ who died for us is indeed Christ who is our life. All our fresh springs are in Him who is risen and "become the first-fruits of them that slept."

The manna was wilderness food; it suited a wilderness journey. It supplied the people's wilderness necessities and continued until the corn was available. There is never any break between God's supplies for His children. There may be moments in outward circumstances when He causes us to wonder and to question what He is doing with us. There may be some moments when our hearts are filled with grief and sorrow, but there is never any pause in the supply of heavenly light from the throne of God.

There is, however, this distinction, that God is always

seeking to lead His children on to new and unexplored areas of the life of redemption in Jesus Christ our Saviour. In order to do that He is always seeking to remove us from the exceptional and the extraordinary, as represented by the manna, to the normal, constant flow of the supplies of His grace in the power of His resurrection. But how reluctant Christian people are to consider the possibility of going on! How reluctant we are to contemplate the possibility of any change in God's dealings with us!

I suppose it is true in this, as in every aspect of life, that the older we get, the less we like the idea of change and the more suspicious we become of it. The old home, the old ways, the old habits, the old friends—they are always the best, and it is so hard to leave them. But there comes a moment in the training of a child of God when the old ways have served God's purpose and have ceased to be a means of discipline to the child's growth in Christian warfare. For always remember, my fellow Christians, that you are far more important to God than the work you do for Him, and that every piece of work He entrusts to you is but the means in His hands of causing you to grow into full conformity to the image of Jesus Christ. Therefore, God is always seeking to lead His children along, to prepare them for change, and to make them ready for new experiences of His grace and power.

Take stock of your life, my friends. Don't be dependent on emotional excitement, spiritual thrills, and spectacular meetings. All these are the evidences of Christian immaturity; they are for the child in the kindergarten. Do you long to be strong for God? Do you long to see Satan put to flight? Then eat of the corn of the land. Jesus fills the hungry with good things; He satisfies the longing soul, and He is yours today for guidance, for discernment of spiritual strategy in attacking the forces of evil in His name. Let your Christian life reach its fruitage through the Cross and draw its power from the throne. Leave the ABC's of the Christian faith and press on until God gives you strength and power through feasting on the Risen Christ and appoints you a warrior in the battle against evil.

Gilgal became a place of realization. The wilderness journey ended, the carnality of that experience over, the food that suited it finished with, the people take of new life in the land of blessing as we take of new resources in our risen Christ.

But I want to show you that Gilgal was something more than that: it was the place of revelation.

Now the Israelites are almost ready for the battle. They have been feasting on the food of the land, but only that they might conquer the enemy in the land. Then Joshua goes out to reconnoiter. Right in front of him lies Jericho, seemingly impregnable, yet it cannot be left behind uncaptured. I picture that general, experienced in wilderness campaigns, asking himself, "How many ladders will I need to scale that wall? And how many battering rams will it take to push over those mighty gates?"

Suddenly appears a man who confronts him and challenges him. But Joshua asks boldly, "Are you for us or for our adversaries?" Who could this man be, with his sword drawn in his hand? The response to Joshua's challenge was crystal clear: "As captain of the host of the Lord am I now come." Without a moment's hesitation Joshua was on his face at the feet of this great Commander. It was in the same words that this very same Commander spoke forty years previously to Moses, saying, "Put thy shoes from off thy

feet, for the place whereon thou standest is holy ground"
(Ex. 3:5).

Surely this was the same One before whom a leper fell and
worshiped in thanksgiving for having been cleansed. Surely
this was none other than the Saviour at whose feet Peter fell
in a fishing boat and acknowledged Him to be his Lord. He
is the One of whom John tells us in the Revelation that He is
"King of kings and Lord of lords." Here is none other than
Jesus Christ, our Lord and Saviour, who has come at that
moment to meet Joshua.

Why has He come? Will He take command in Joshua's
place? Will He take over Joshua's authority? Perhaps, but
certainly not primarily. He has come, He says, as captain of
the host of the Lord, and "the host of the Lord" did not refer
to the people camped at Gilgal, but to an unseen army, in-
visible to the human eye, that surrounds the throne of God
from all eternity and is ready to obey His commands and
conduct operations in heavenly places against a satanic foe.

Several times in God's Word we read of that host. Jacob
saw it when he came back from exile. Elisha's servant saw it
when he was trapped by the armies of Syria and beheld
around him a host of heavenly beings who were to take up
the cudgels on his behalf. The Lord Jesus spoke of it when
He was leaving Gethsemane—the twelve legions of angels
who at that moment were at His disposal, who at one whisper from Him would have rent the heavens and destroyed
His foes. Is not the whole story of the Bible the account, on
the one hand, of the spiritual forces of evil who control this
world and, on the other hand, of the spiritual forces of light
who, when Jesus shall come again, shall destroy every foe
and cast them down into hell?

When Joshua worshiped before this great Commander

and fell at His feet, allied himself with the Commander's power and accepted His leadership in this attack on the enemy, was it any wonder that the walls of Jericho fell without a battle being fought? Was it any wonder that whole armies fled before Joshua and the land of Canaan was captured in seven years? These were but the earthly, visible results of victories won in heavenly places with angelic forces. Jericho's walls collapsed without a shot being fired, so to speak, because Joshua had allied himself in worship and in surrender to this Captain of the host of the Lord.

Gilgal was a place of revelation. Oh that the Holy Spirit would write this word on your heart and mine and help us to understand it, so that we may know the true character of our warfare and the secret of our victory!

Behind the vast powers of ungodly empires and rulers in this world today, behind 800 million people committed unto death to the power of Communism, is Satanic authority. Behind the hardness of hearts against the truth and the indifference of men and women to the gospel of Christ is the god of this world, who has blinded the minds of those who believe not. Behind the resistance of wife, husband, children or parents to the Word of God; behind the divided home, the broken heart, the ruined life, and the shattered testimony is Satan, who in these last days of grace is turning on all his power, for he knows that his time is short.

Behind the rapidly closing doors to missionary service, behind the failure of many missionaries to stand the test of health and strength and spirit, behind the evacuation right and left of one mission station after another, behind the shortage of money to keep missionaries on the field, behind all this is Satan, who has gripped the hearts and the pockets of God's people and held them, as it were, in a vice.

Let us acknowledge this in the presence of God—it is either revival or ruin for us all!

What is our answer to a need on that scale and of that character? What do we attempt to do? We put forth herculean efforts, thinking of this method and that which will attract people to our churches. We plan exciting advertising and give away prizes. We spend vast sums of money to bring people under the sound of the gospel. And when it is all over, we retire from the fight—weary, baffled, disappointed, and perplexed.

What *can* we do? We have put forth every effort under the sun. We have placarded our cities with advertisements and launched great campaigns. But, apart from a few here and a few there, the results are tragically lacking. In this generation Satan seems to be capturing millions for himself in comparison with the hundreds that come to Jesus Christ.

However, "the weapons of our warfare are not carnal, but mighty through God to the pulling down of strong holds" (II Cor. 10:4). May the Holy Spirit enlighten you to understand this word and to let it grip your heart. All through His lifetime here the Lord Jesus encountered these same spiritual enemies. They assailed Him in the wilderness; they concentrated their forces on Him in Gethsemane; they launched a full-scale attack on the Cross, and said, "If thou be the Son of God, come down." But in His death He resisted them and triumphed over them. He ascended through all their ranks, defied their authority, and stripped them from Himself as He ascended to the place of absolute supremacy far above them all. "And God hath put [not, please note, "will put," but *hath put*] all his foes under his feet, and God hath given him [Jesus] to be the head of all things to the church, which is the fulness of him who filleth all in all" (Eph. 1:22, 23).

God forgive us that we are attempting today to fight spiritual enemies by carnal means. It cannot be done. May He forgive us when we seem to think that by planning, publicity, advertising, campaigning and working we will attain something, whereas, in point of fact, we achieve nothing. Have we not understood that the weapons of our warfare are not carnal?

Are you committed one hundred per cent to living a holy life? Have you determined to put away all revealed sin? Have you determined to ally yourself by faith with the Christ of absolute authority? If you have, once again the Church of the Lord Jesus Christ can take up the sword and, in the language of the Old Testament, brandish it and say, "The sword of the Lord and of Gideon." "I will build my church," said the Lord Jesus, "and the gates of hell shall not prevail against it" (Matt. 16:18).

An ordinary girl, sitting at a typewriter in her office and thinking she is not able to do much about the Lord's work, can, if she is linked with the Lord in heaven, give testimony that is irresistible. A man who works in a factory five days a week, amid obscene and blasphemous company and almost in despair that nothing ever seems to happen for the Lord, may realize that faith is not only looking back to Calvary but also looking up to the throne, and so begin to derive heavenly power and to count for God.

To an uneducated boy or girl, trying to teach a little handful of youngsters in Sunday school and wondering how it can be done, may come a moment in experience when he or she is linked with the living Christ on His throne, and God begins to work and the Jerichos to fall.

To a simple housewife whose husband has refused for years to accept Christ, and whose home has been divided, may come one day the realization that her faith is in an omnipotent Lord, and that faith linked to omnipotence becomes mighty and powerful. Then God begins to do what He could not do for a lifetime, and the man is saved.

All that God asks from us is to take the Lord Jesus Christ into the heart of the church so that every member of it may be linked with the throne. If we are made captive by a living Christ, then God begins to work. Revival comes, and lives are blessed. So souls are saved, and the church moves on like a mighty army!

# CHAPTER 8

# CELEBRATING VICTORY

## JOSHUA 6:23

*Now Jericho was straitly shut up because of the children of Israel: none went out, and none came in.*

*And the Lord said unto Joshua, See, I have given into thine hand Jericho, and the king thereof, and the mighty men of valour.*

*And ye shall compass the city, all ye men of war, and go round about the city once. Thus shalt thou do six days.*

*And seven priests shall bear before the ark seven trumpets of rams' horns: and the seventh day ye shall compass the city seven times, and the priests shall blow with the trumpets.*

*And it shall come to pass, that when they make a long blast with the ram's horn, and when ye hear the sound of the trumpet, all the people shall shout with a great shout; and the wall of the city shall fall down flat, and the people shall ascend up every man straight before him.*

*And Joshua the son of Nun called the priests, and said unto them, Take up the ark of the covenant, and let seven priests bear seven trumpets of rams' horns before the ark of the Lord.*

*And he said unto the people, Pass on, and compass the*

*city, and let him that is armed pass on before the ark of the Lord.*

*And it came to pass, when Joshua had spoken unto the people, that the seven priests bearing the seven trumpets of rams' horns passed on before the Lord, and blew with the trumpets: and the ark of the covenant of the Lord followed them.*

*And the armed men went before the priests that blew with the trumpets, and the rereward came after the ark, the priests going on, and blowing with the trumpets.*

*And Joshua had commanded the people, saying, Ye shall not shout, nor make any noise with your voice, neither shall any word proceed out of your mouth, until the day I bid you shout; then shall ye shout.*

*So the ark of the Lord compassed the city, going about it once: and they came into the camp, and lodged in the camp.*

*And Joshua rose up early in the morning, and the priests took up the ark of the Lord.*

*And seven priests bearing seven trumpets of rams' horns before the ark of the Lord went on continually, and blew with the trumpets: and the armed men went before them; but the rereward came after the ark of the Lord, the priests going on, and blowing with the trumpets.*

*And the second day they compassed the city once, and returned into the camp: so they did six days.*

*And it came to pass on the seventh day, that they rose early about the dawning of the day, and compassed the city after the same manner seven times: only on that day they compassed the city seven times.*

*And it came to pass at the seventh time, when the priests blew with trumpets, Joshua said unto the people, Shout; for the Lord hath given you the city.*

*And the city shall be accursed, even it, and all that are therein, to the Lord: only Rahab the harlot shall live, she and all that are with her in the house, because she hid the messengers that we sent.*

*And ye, in any wise keep yourselves from the accursed thing, lest ye make yourselves accursed, when ye take of the accursed thing, and make the camp of Israel a curse, and trouble it.*

*But all the silver, and gold, and vessels of brass and iron, are consecrated unto the Lord: they shall come into the treasury of the Lord.*

*So the people shouted when the priests blew with the trumpets: and it came to pass, when the people heard the sound of the trumpet, and the people shouted with a great shout, that the wall fell down flat, so that the people went up into the city, every man straight before him, and they took the city.*

JOSHUA 6: 1–20

We have been studying the principles of release from the bondage of the kingdom of Satan. Deliverance is always through the blood of the Cross and through the Lamb that was slain. As the Israelites were led out of their slavery in Egypt, so are we delivered out of the kingdom of Satan into the kingdom of God.

Alas, in our Christian life we have traversed, we acknowledge, far too long a wilderness journey, in which we have known in a measure the presence of God and His victory and also many defeats and failures. Some have crossed over Jordan, the place of our oneness with Christ in His death and resurrection, where we came to understand that He is in us to be our life and our victory, and to meet our every need.

We are on redemption ground. But the Christian who comes through the wilderness into the land of full salvation discovers to his amazement that immediately Jericho confronts him. How Christian people have been baffled by this experience!

Let no one imagine that there is a state of grace in which they are utterly free from all the wiles of Satan, that there is some experience that enables him to be finished with the whole battle of sin and temptation. The Word of God and human experience are opposed to that viewpoint, and any child of God who has based his hope on that kind of experience will live to be shattered and disillusioned. For he will discover that, though he has claimed his place with Christ in His death and resurrection believing every day of his life that Christ is his victory, yet before him rises a Jericho.

Satan, who bound him when he was in Egypt and attacked him in the wilderness, comes with increasing force and ever-increasing subtlety when the child of God finds himself in the land of blessing. Have you taken your place in death to yourself at the Cross and in risen life with our precious Lord, and today are claiming your inheritance, Christ your victory, but you are bewildered to discover that right in your path lies Jericho?

To some, Jericho may be a force from within their own personality—some weakness of temperament or weakness of character. Most of us know that there is a weak spot in our makeup. Maybe it is something we learned as children, which has followed us and often conquered us through our adolescence and youth into mature years. Each one knows well enough there is a place where he has to set a special guard—for there is Jericho.

It may be that the Jericho in your life is something outside of yourself—perhaps an impossible situation in your family circle and in your home life. Is there something that seems to keep you right back from doing what you honestly believe to be the will of God? Time and time again, God has spoken to you, maybe, about serving Him on the mission field or in some special sphere of opportunity, and yet always between you and the will of God there is a Jericho. It stands there week by week, and it baffles and mocks you, for you are conscious all the time that it is holding you back from being the man or the woman that you long to be.

How is this city to be overcome?

What a strange spectacle it must have been for the inhabitants of Jericho to see the Israelites encircle the great fortifications of the city daily in absolute silence! The only sound that reached the walls was the sound of the trumpets blown by the priests, who were at the head of the procession, with the Ark of the Covenant in the center, and the people of God falling in behind. I can well imagine that the silence of the army was often broken by the taunts of the people who watched behind the walls.

The opening verses of chapter 6 tell us, however, that though they jeered, the people of Jericho were stricken with fear. They had observed something about the spiritual resources of these invaders that had caused them to be panic-stricken, though the tactics of encircling the wall seemed to be stupid and ridiculous beyond words. In the midst of their scoffing there was dread of the army that walked so silently around the walls.

To the Israelites, Jericho still remained the same when they came back to their tents night after night, and on the seventh day, when they circled the wall seven times. Then, on the completion of no less than thirteen tours around

Jericho, at the command of Joshua the trumpets were blown and the people shouted with a great shout. The walls of Jericho fell down flat, and every man went straight up before him, all converging on the center of the city. In modern terms, Jericho was captured without a shot being fired.

Has that a counterpart in Christian experience? What does it teach you about the way God delivers His people and about the way He can see you through to conquer the Jericho which confronts you in personal life?

How was this city captured? It was not subdued by mechanical means or by human methods. "By faith the walls of Jericho fell down, after they were compassed about seven days," says the inspired commentary in Hebrews 11:30.

Observe with me carefully one or two things about the faith that caused those walls to collapse. You will notice how the Israelites' faith was tested. Thirteen times they walked around the city, though no reason had been given them why they should. The whole situation had been explained in detail to Joshua, and he knew exactly what God was doing, but the people did not; he gave them instructions only for that day. I suppose that the hardest thing for the people to do was to keep quiet—to walk around in silence. But at last Joshua commanded them to shout, and at their shout of victory the walls fell down.

Notice that the central feature of the procession was the Ark of the Covenant—it is mentioned eleven times in this chapter. This was the symbol of the Israelites' faith. They were able to walk around the city in silence because, even though they did not know what God was doing, God was with them. The Ark had brought them through Jordan; it had been the symbol of their past experiences of the power of God. If you read the chapter you will find that the eleventh verse tell us that "the ark of the Lord encompassed the city." Yes, God walked around Jericho with the Israelites thirteen times before the word was spoken by their commander. "Shout," said Joshua, "for the Lord hath given you the city." In answer to that shout, in response to the blowing of the trumpet, the walls collapsed, and the people marched through victorious.

Why had they walked thirteen times around that place in silence? I suggest it took that long for every one of them to realize that it was utterly impossible for them to capture Jericho if God were not with them—thirteen big long looks at the enemy, until they became convinced that they were no match for those behind the walls. God made the Israelites walk around the great fortification until within themselves they died to every hope of conquest unless God should intervene.

Is there a counterpart in our experience? You are conscious that God has brought you along in the Christian life and manifested Himself in blessing to you, but there is still the Jericho that haunts you: the Jericho within your human personality, or the Jericho outside.

The greatest difficulty in the Christian life is to get to the place where one is prepared to admit that the whole thing is too big for him, and that the power of the enemy is too great for him, and if his Jericho is to fall, then, somehow, God must bring it about. I believe that before God entrusts any of His people with a real measure of spiritual power, victory, and blessing, He brings them to a place from where they have surveyed Jericho so long that they have come to see that its conquest is absolutely hopeless. God expects nothing more from us than failure, yet we spend years trying to make ourselves something other than a failure. So long as we think we can do it alone, the omnipotent resources of God in Jesus Christ our Risen Lord cannot help us.

Another one of the biggest tests in Christian experience is the test of silence. How we long to talk about our difficulties to others, to get Christians to help us through in prayer, to share our burdens with a friend. What a moment in the Christian life it is when the soul comes to realize that our expectation is from God, when the truth begins to dawn on us that it is not what I achieve, but the victory that I take from God in Christ Jesus, who died and rose again that He might give it to me!

That Jericho of yours will stand in front of you until there comes a moment in your life when you understand that Jericho is God's gift to you in Christ. The victory over it is yours to take, but God will give it to you only when you get to the place in Christian experience where you fully admit in His presence that you are utterly unable to take it yourself.

But, in thinking of these simple lessons of victory, I want more especially to give this text its proper place in all the revelation of God's Word. I would lift it out of the narrow realm of the personal and individual, and show you the tremendous Jerichos which stand in the way of the people of God as a whole. There is the Jericho of sin. There is the Jericho of indifference. There is the Jericho of materialism. There is the Jericho of paganism. Worse than that, there is the Jericho within the church of disloyal Christians, of unconsecrated lives, of people who have become so used to sinners going to hell that they don't care. Surrounding the Church of God today and within her walls stand endless Jerichos which seem to be utterly unconquerable.

Perhaps we have been around these Jerichos often enough

in our experience. We have fought against them; we have tried this method and that method. We have tried to batter them down with our preaching, with our publicity, with our efforts and our talking, but the Jerichos are still there We have come in despair to the realization that the Jerichos that confront the church ought to be taken, and that only a new visitation from heaven of the power of God in Holy Ghost revival can touch them. I wonder how long we as a Christian people have been trying to scale the walls of these Jerichos by sitting down in committees and thinking out this method and that. We forget that God doesn't want new methods; He wants new men.

The burden on my heart is this, that surrounding us throughout the world are Jerichos which stand and mock at our efforts. They laugh at our weak attempts to reach the world in this day and to complete the task of evangelism to bring back the King. The Church of the Lord Jesus Christ today is in a desperate situation; it is losing ground rapidly. I am not concerned about what you say of the impact made here and there by the gospel, I ask you to look into your own life, look around your own circle of fellowship, and look up to heaven and say, "Lord, we are absolutely helpless."

Do you know that there are more unsaved people in the world today than there ever have been? Do you know that there are 1,500 million people who have never heard the gospel? Do you know that today behind the Iron Curtain men and women are being massacred for their faith in Jesus? Do you know that thirty million people die every year— 3,400 people an hour going into eternity? Let us not be afraid to face this fact, that unless God visits us in sovereign power with Holy Ghost revival the church today is beaten.

How should we seek to deal with these Jerichos? **The**

Israelites walked around Jericho thirteen times and never said a word—they could afford to. Why? Because the people in Jericho were terrified of them. Let that lesson of Jericho ring in your hearts. The Israelites could afford to walk around those walls, to do the thing that God told them to do, and to be utterly silent, because they knew that God was in their midst and that the enemy within the walls of Jericho was terror-stricken.

In those sentences, for the Spirit-discerning man or woman, I have exposed the tragedy of 20th-century Christianity. For lack of real evidence of the supernatural in the church we cannot afford to be silent—we have to shout. We have to join the commercial interests that line up before the radio to advertise their tooth pastes and their chewing gum, for the man who shouts loudest will get the biggest listening public. The Lord was not in the wind, or in the earthquake, or in the fire, but in the still small voice. Surely the church is on the wrong foot altogether and we are attacking the situation with wrong methods when we try to match a spiritual need with carnal expedients. It is impossible to achieve a heavenly task with the use of Hollywood technique; we inevitably fail.

Are you prepared, committee member, to rethink the program of your particular group and scrap it if it is not of God? Are you honestly prepared to stand firm in fellowship with others that you may give God an opportunity to speak and to direct the course of your testimony? Are you truly prepared to give God the right to change you, or do you love your ways and your methods so much that you dare not abandon them? The answer to your Jerichos is on your knees—nowhere else. That is not inactivity or passivity;

it is linking yourself in your weakness and your helplessness with the omnipotent power of God.

When people wait on God and listen for His voice, and travail in prayer, then the enemy begins to get afraid. Then there will be those here and there who will come under what the Old Book calls conviction of sin. That is what is lacking. We seem to imagine today that our religion is to be simply another form of entertainment.

How much do we know about real conviction of sin? When that sinks into a man's consciousness and makes him see where he is in God's sight, I tell you there is no relationship that matters but the relationship with Him. Everything else fades into insignificance; we are broken before God, waiting for the cleansing and delivering and infilling power of the Holy Spirit, or else our service is finished.

What about those who delight in sowing discord among the brethren? What about those who are worldly? What about those who just don't care? What about those who never think about coming to a prayer meeting? Have you ever stopped to think that prayerlessness in the sight of God is a desperate sin in His children? Nothing can touch this world except heaven-sent conviction of sin, and God convicts the world in the measure in which God convicts the church. Has He convicted us?

But I must turn to a note of victory. Every Jericho in the world will fall. I believe it with all my heart.

How did Jericho fall? There were the shouts; there was the sound of the trumpets. Listen to these wonderful words: "The Lord himself shall descend from heaven with a shout . . . with the trump of God" (I Thess. 4:16). The world, with all its sin and all its corruption, will crumble at the revelation of Jesus Christ! "And I John saw the holy city, new

Jerusalem, coming down from God out of heaven, prepared as a bride adorned for her husband. . . . And God shall wipe away all tears from their eyes" (Rev. 21:2, 4). Can it be that this glorious day is nearer than we think? Can it be that the Lord is waiting to get His people broken and repentant and humble, in that condition in which they can shout for the coming of the King?

It may be at morn, when the day is awaking,
When sunlight thro' darkness and shadow is breaking,
That Jesus will come in the fullness of glory,
To receive from the world "His own."

It may be at midday, it may be at twilight;
It may be, perchance, that the blackness of midnight
Will burst into light in the blaze of His glory,
When Jesus receives "His own."

O Lord Jesus, how long, how long
Ere we shout the glad song?
Christ returneth; hallelujah!
Hallelujah! Amen.

# CHAPTER 9

# SETBACKS—THEIR CAUSE AND CURE

## JOSHUA 7:13

*But the children of Israel committed a trespass in the accursed thing: for Achan, the son of Carmi, the son of Zabdi the son of Zerah, of the tribe of Judah, took of the accursed thing: and the anger of the Lord was kindled against the children of Israel.*

*And Joshua sent men from Jericho to Ai, which is beside Bethaven, on the east side of Bethel, and spake unto them, saying, Go up and view the country. And the men went up and viewed Ai.*

*And they returned to Joshua, and said unto him, Let not all the people go up; but let about two or three thousand men go up and smite Ai; and make not all the people to labour thither; for they are but few.*

*So there went up thither of the people about three thousand men: and they fled before the men of Ai.*

*And the men of Ai smote of them about thirty and six men: for they chased them from before the gate even unto Shebarim, and smote them in the going down: wherefore the hearts of the people melted, and became as water.*

*And Joshua rent his clothes, and fell to the earth upon his face before the ark of the Lord until the eventide, he and the elders of Israel, and put dust upon their heads.*

*And Joshua said, Alas, O Lord God, wherefore hast thou at all brought this people over Jordan, to deliver us into the hand of the Amorites, to destroy us? would to God we had been content, and dwelt on the other side Jordan!*

*O Lord, what shall I say, when Israel turneth their backs before their enemies!*

*For the Canaanites and all the inhabitants of the land shall hear of it, and shall environ us round, and cut off our name from the earth: and what wilt thou do unto thy great name?*

*And the Lord said unto Joshua, Get thee up; wherefore liest thou thus upon thy face?*

*Israel hath sinned, and they have also transgressed my covenant which I commanded them: for they have even taken of the accursed thing, and have also stolen, and dissembled also, and they have put it even among their own stuff.*

*Therefore the children of Israel could not stand before their enemies, but turned their backs before their enemies, because they were accursed: neither will I be with you any more, except ye destroy the accursed from among you.*

*Up, sanctify the people, and say, Sanctify yourselves against tomorrow: for thus saith the Lord God of Israel, There is an accursed thing in the midst of thee, O Israel: thou canst not stand before thine enemies, until ye take away the accursed thing from among you.*

*In the morning therefore ye shall be brought according to your tribes: and it shall be, that the tribe which the Lord taketh shall come according to the families thereof; and the family which the Lord shall take shall come by households;*

*and the household which the Lord shall take shall come man by man.*

*And it shall be, that he that is taken with the accursed thing shall be burnt with fire, he and all that he hath: because he hath transgressed the covenant of the Lord, and because he hath wrought folly in Israel.*

*So Joshua rose up early in the morning, and brought Israel by their tribes; and the tribe of Judah was taken:*

*And he brought the family of Judah; and he took the family of the Zarhites: and he brought the family of the Zarhites man by man; and Zabdi was taken:*

*And he brought his household man by man; and Achan, the son of Carmi, the son of Zabdi, the son of Zerah, of the tribe of Judah, was taken.*

*And Joshua said unto Achan, My son, give, I pray thee, glory to the Lord God of Israel, and make confession unto him; and tell me now what thou hast done; hide it not from me.*

*And Achan answered Joshua, and said, Indeed I have sinned against the Lord God of Israel, and thus and thus have I done:*

*When I saw among the spoils a goodly Babylonish garment, and two hundred shekels of silver, and a wedge of gold of fifty shekels weight, then I coveted them, and took them; and, behold, they are hid in the earth in the midst of my tent, and the silver under it.*

*So Joshua sent messengers, and they ran unto the tent; and, behold, it was hid in his tent, and the silver under it.*

*And they took them out of the midst of the tent; and brought them unto Joshua, and unto all the children of Israel, and laid them out before the Lord.*

*And Joshua, and all Israel with him, took Achan the son*

*of Zerah, and the silver, and the garment, and the wedge of*
*gold, and his sons, and his daughters, and his oxen, and his*
*asses, and his sheep, and his tent, and all that he had: and they*
*brought them unto the valley of Achor.*

*And Joshua said, Why hast thou troubled us? the Lord*
*shall trouble thee this day. And all Israel stoned him with*
*stones, and burned them with fire, after they had stoned*
*them with stones.*

*And they raised over him a great heap of stones unto this*
*day. So the Lord turned from the fierceness of his anger.*
*Wherefore the name of that place was called, The Valley of*
*Achor, unto this day.*

JOSHUA 7:1–26

The seventh chapter of the book of Joshua opens with an
ominous "But . . ."

So far, the people of God have been completely victorious
in crossing the Jordan, in entering the land, in dealing with
God at Gilgal, and at Jericho. So far all the story has been a
story of success. But here we find the children of Israel in full
retreat. We find Joshua on his face before God, filled with
dismay.

He had counted on unbroken victory in the land; he felt
sure that there would be no more defeat, that never again
would his people Israel fail. It appeared now that either God
had deserted them or else even God Himself was unable to
cope with the powerful enemy in the land of Canaan. Israel
seemed to be in desperate peril. Obviously their strength and
resource in themselves were quite inadequate to defeat the
armies of Canaan. They had only established a bridgehead
in the land, and it seemed as if they well might be flung right
back into the river Jordan.

Even worse, what discredit would attach to the name of the Lord if that happened! "O Lord," cried Joshua, "what wilt thou do unto thy great name?" His chief concern was not that Israel had been defeated, but that the name of Jehovah had been dishonored.

Unbroken victory for His people was certainly God's purpose. The defeat at Ai, the account of which is contained in this seventh chapter of Joshua, was the only defeat they suffered in their conquest of the land of Canaan. Defeat in Canaan might occur, but it need not.

A life of unbroken victory over sin is the purpose of God for every child of His redeemed by the blood of Christ. However, God does not make it impossible for His children to sin: He always makes it possible for them *not* to sin. Defeat may happen in the life of the Christian, but it need not.

Of course, the child of God who has pressed forward into the land of full salvation and is claiming the victory that is his in Jesus Christ is in more acute danger of defeat than he who has not gone so far. The child of God who is determined to live his life in the center of the will of God ceases to live, as it were, in the shelter of the valley. He is exposed now; he is on higher ground, where the storms lash with all their fury. Because of his determination to be content with nothing less than God's best, such a man of God is more than ever subject to the subtlety of the devil—a first-class target for him, indeed.

Defeat, I say again, need not happen, but it may. And if it does, it is essential at that moment to discover the reasons for failure and to seek there and then to remove them. I want briefly to examine with you the reasons for failure at Ai, and I think that in doing this we shall expose some of the reasons why we all have failed in our Christian lives.

The first reason for failure at Ai, this defeat of the armies of Israel, was, manifestly, self-confidence. It was only a small city compared to Jericho, which lay in ruins, and it seemed quite unnecessary for the whole army to attack it. A few thousand men would be sufficient, said those who had reconnoitered. They reported to Joshua, "Ai is quite insignificant. Don't trouble the whole army, just send two or three thousand men."

That argument was based on the supposition that Israel had captured Jericho. Actually, all they had done was to walk around the walls and shout; it was God who had taken the city. The silence which reigned over the ruins of Jericho was not a testimony to the strength of the people of God, but a testimony to the power of Jehovah Himself. To argue as the children of Israel did at Ai was to suppose that now, because of Jericho, some quality of greatness and strength had been imparted to them which would stand them in good stead throughout all their future campaigning.

Mark this lesson well in your own Christian life: there is no experience in Christian living so full of danger as the flush of victory. There is no moment so perilous as when, for the first time in his Christian life, the man of God has experienced deliverance from sin. At such times we begin to take pride in ourselves, and to boast that our own arm has saved us. We so easily imagine that because we have achieved victory once, God has imparted to us some new strength which will see us through all our earthly journey.

Alas, how utterly contradictory to the truth that is! The fact is that, apart from the grace of God and the blood of Jesus, the smallest temptations will be too powerful for us. The victories we win in fellowship with a Risen Christ impart no strength to us. The victory you won yesterday will not bring you power today. The greatest lesson that the child of God has to learn is the lesson learned by Paul, that "in my flesh dwelleth no good thing," that "when I am weak, then am I strong"; for the greatest cause of failure in Christian living is just this: imagining that the victory God has given us has imparted strength to us to win every battle, when it has done nothing of the kind. Remember, fellow Christian, the first reason for failure at Ai was self-confidence.

The second reason for the failure of Israel at Ai was, manifestly, neglect of prayer. It is quite clear, from the reading of the second verse, that Joshua at this moment failed to wait on God. He did not go back to Gilgal. Flushed with the victory at Jericho, he immediately made plans to capture the next portion of the territory. Had he prostrated himself in humility at the time when the people shouted for victory at Jericho, he would never have been humbled to the dust over the defeat at Ai. If only he had sought God's counsel at the moment of triumph, he would have discerned immediately that there was sin in camp. Failure to pray always makes us insensitive to sin.

If you pray in time of victory you will never have to plead in a time of defeat. Indeed, to plead with God in the time of defeat was useless: now was the time to do something about it. "Why liest thou thus upon thy face?" was the rebuke Joshua heard from God. This was not the time for prayer; it was the time for action, for the ruthless extermination of sin. If at the hour of victory Joshua had humbled himself before God, he would have had revealed to him that he was heading straight for disaster unless he dealt with something that lay deep in the heart of the people.

One of the greatest temptations that can come to you after you have proved that God is able to give you victory, is to neglect to pray. When you think that you are strong and don't need to pray any more, then you will have dulled your sensitiveness to sin. It is only prayer in the hour of victory that makes a man of God realize that he will face defeat again unless he maintains continuous contact with the Lord Jesus Christ. The moment of victory is the moment for humiliation. When one experiences the excitement and thrill of God giving him a new deliverance from sin, that should be the moment, not for pride, but for humility.

I wonder how many of us as Christian people have gone out to defeat and disillusionment in Christian life because we didn't pray—when our senses were dulled, and we were no longer acutely conscious of the fact that sin was still there, and that Satan would gain the upper hand unless we clung to the Lord Jesus Christ.

The third reason for Israel's defeat at Ai was disobedience. What a striking statement we find in verse 11. God speaks to Joshua and says, "Israel has sinned; . . . they have taken of the devoted thing" (RV). Where the Authorized version says "accursed"; the Revised Version says "devoted"—something set apart for God.

Now mark well a lesson here for all time. What actually had happened? One man had stolen property which belonged to God, had taken of the spoils of victory that were to be set apart for the Lord. One individual in the camp had betrayed God's trust, and the verdict from heaven was not, "Achan hath sinned," but "Israel hath sinned." One man had failed, and the whole army was defeated. You see, the children of Israel were a nation—they were brought to redemption ground as one man, the weakest of them and the strongest of them. They were a complete entity; God was dealing with them as a corporate body through whom His purposes for men were to be fulfilled. Here at Ai, therefore, the verdict of heaven on the sin of one member of the community was, "Israel hath sinned."

I trust that the Holy Spirit is going to write this lesson deeply on your hearts. Where one member of a local fellowship is guilty before God of sin, the verdict from heaven is, "My people have sinned." When one man steps out of blessing and does something contrary to God's will, the verdict of the all-searching eye of our Master is, "My people have sinned."

No individual Christian can sin without affecting the whole church. No child of God can grow cold in his spiritual life without lowering the temperature of everybody else around him. The victory of the whole community depends on the victorious life of every individual church member. Let no Christian ever think that because he is not doing some specific task for the Lord he does not matter. Let nobody imagine that he can be lost in a crowd and be forgotten. Let me say that the testimony of your church in its community and throughout the world depends on the victorious life of every man and woman on your church rolls. The witness of our church to the glory of God is affected by the testimony of every one of us. If only we would realize that, how readily we would recognize the need for helping and strengthening and praying for each other on the pilgrim journey. The unity of the Spirit and the bond of peace are the testimony of victory in the house of God.

There were three reasons for defeat at Ai: self-confidence, prayerlessness, and disobedience. Can it be that some Christian who has entered into a new experience of God and claimed by faith the victory of Christ has been disillusioned and defeated? And can it be that the reason for this is that he has been confident in himself, has not prayed, or has been disobedient to God?

But I must ask you to look at the most important thing of all, for after we determine the cause of such a setback, let us see that we understand the cure.

What was it that ultimately brought victory at Ai? First of all, there was confession. Somehow, I feel with Achan as he watched the army of God in full retreat, for he knew perfectly well that he had something in his own house belonging to God which he had stolen for himself. And when he saw those thirty-six men dead on the battlefield it became increasingly clear to his poor wretched conscience that he was responsible. And when, as recorded in the 21st verse of this chapter, he faced the court which Joshua had appointed to try him, his story was, "Joshua, I saw, I coveted, I took. It was the lust of the flesh, the lust of the eyes, the pride of life. I acknowledge that I am guilty." Under the burden of his guilt his collapse was complete.

I wonder if you and I have ever truly faced what sin is and understood its far-reaching effect. Somebody says to me "I have never been guilty of Achan's sin." Haven't you? Have you touched the life of another child of God and marred it? Has your influence on some friend been so shattering that he will never be the same again? Have you taken of the property of the Lord for yourself? That was Achan's sin—"I saw, I desired, I took, and I held." Christian, has that been your failure? Have you soiled some life with sinful hands and sinful influence, and then tried to cover up the consequences? That is what Achan did. All of us are more afraid of being found out than ashamed of the sin in our hearts. Our first reaction to the prick of conscience is always to plan that, somehow, our sin may not become known. But one day the net is drawn around us, one day the sin is exposed, and the Holy Spirit says, "Thou art guilty." Then, in humility be fore God and often before His people, we have to say, "Lord Jesus, I saw, I desired, I took, and I held."

For his great sin Achan and all his family were destroyed. What tremendous punishment! How often these verses have been quoted to me by people who believe that the God of the New Testament is not the God of the Old, who say they could never worship or believe in a God who would be responsible for the destruction of this man and his whole family. It brings a sense of horror to my own heart as I contemplate the loathing of my God and Saviour of everything that is sinful, and His determination to wipe out from my life and experience what is contrary to His will.

The only way to deal with the evil that was bringing defeat to Israel and dishonor to the name of the Lord was to blot it out. In the light of God's Word, to acknowledge that we have been guilty is not enough. Have you ever spent an hour asking yourself, "Why did it happen? What was the cause of it? Need it have happened? Why did I allow it? I didn't pray, I was proud, I was disobedient." You have to go back to where you failed, where you can see the weakness in your life. When you get to the very root of it, you need to look up into the face of Jesus and acknowledge, "I saw, I coveted, I took," and then you can thank Him that "if we confess our sin, he is faithful and just to forgive us our sin, and to cleanse us from all unrighteousness" (I John 1:9).

All that Christians are asked to do to cleanse themselves of guilt is to confess and forsake their sin. "Wherefore take unto you the whole armor of God, that you may be able to withstand in the evil day, and having done all, to stand" (Eph. 6:13).

But the Word of God says, also, "Thou canst not stand before thine enemies until ye take away the accursed thing from among you" (Joshua 7:13).

My fellow believers, in the name of the Lord Jesus Christ I bid you, with all the love I have in my heart for you, either get right with God or leave His house. Maybe some subtractions from the membership roll would be the first step toward victory in many a church. I pray God that, whatever it may cost you in terms of personal humiliation before Him and before men, you will search out any Achan in your own life —don't bother about other people—and get right with God. In the presence of the Lord Jesus give up your sin and claim the cleansing of His blood.

# Chapter 10

# THE CHRISTIAN LAW OF LIBERTY

### JOSHUA 8:30

*And he wrote there upon the stones a copy of the law of Moses, which he wrote in the presence of the children of Israel.*

*And all Israel, and their elders, and officers, and their judges, on this side the ark and on that side before the priests the Levites, which bare the ark of the covenant of the Lord, as well the stranger, as he that was born among them; half of them over against mount Gerizim, and half of them over against mount Ebal; as Moses the servant of the Lord had commanded before, that they should bless the people of Israel.*

*And afterward he read all the words of the law, the blessings and cursings, according to all that is written in the book of the law.*

*There was not a word of all that Moses commanded, which Joshua read not before all the congregation of Israel, with the women, and the little ones, and the strangers that were conversant among them.*

JOSHUA 8:32–35

Much of Chapter 8 of the book of Joshua is a record of the ultimate victory at Ai after the humiliating experience of defeat. I could not pass over this particular portion without recommending that you read the story of the strategy which Joshua had to adopt in order to recover the ground that had been lost. You would read of planned withdrawal, of pretended defeat, of an ambush which had to be laid, and of an enemy who was tricked into thinking that he was victorious. You would read the account of how every able man was flung into the battle line of Israel in order that Ai should be finally conquered. Ai was much less formidable than Jericho, but after the experience of defeat it was much more difficult to overcome.

If you were to sit down alone with your Bible and reflect on that record, I believe you would find yourself indelibly impressed with the fact that the recovery of lost ground in Christian experience is the most difficult problem of all. Thirty minutes of wilful disobedience in the life of a child of God has often resulted in thirty years of being out of blessing. Some man, after twelve months of intensive Christian activity, has laid down his duties for a little while and gone to a summer camp for vacation. There he has become entangled in a friendship which he knows is out of the will of God and contrary to the teaching of the Word of God, and that man's Christian service has been damaged for years because of it. Lost ground is mighty hard to regain, and if that lesson could be seared with a hot iron on your conscience, you would find it more difficult than at present you do to slip into wilful sin.

Many a man has grown into middle life with no vision for a perishing world, with no burden for a lost soul, and no real heart in the work he does for God. If he were to ask himself why, he could look back into his youth to a time when, for a few moments, he had turned away from God's best, when he had been led into an unholy practice and because of that had lost his grip and his power. The Holy Spirit was grieved, and now the man is a useless instrument for God—still preaching, still teaching, still leading, but out of blessing. May the Holy Spirit write it with power on your hearts: lost ground in Christian living is very hard to recover.

This is the essential background on which this chapter is based. The people of God experienced at Ai the difficulty of recovering lost ground, and what happened immediately afterward was to be expected. No sooner had they slipped up and been beaten, and recovered ground, than there was written on their minds the principles by which they might possess all that God had for them in the land of Canaan. Here was the secret of insuring that the same disaster might not happen again.

They went for a thirty-mile pilgrimage to the valley of Shechem, one of the loveliest vales in Palestine. There, so to speak, they were taught the law of liberty. They were taught the place that the law of God must have in their lives as inhabitants of the land. They were taught the way by which they would be blessed and the way by which they would be cursed, and it was shown them that there was no alternative: it must either be life or death.

Let me remind you, my fellow Christians, that there *are* laws in the Christian life, rules which we are expected to keep. Was it not Paul's great concern lest, having preached to others, he himself might be a castaway? Or, to use the paraphrase of a modern translation: "Lest, having proclaimed the rules to other people, I myself should be disqualified" (I Cor. 9:27)? Here in the closing verses of

Chapter 8 of Joshua are set out for us the principles of Christian living, the law of liberty in the Christian life.

What a lovely valley Shechem was! This was not the first time that a dramatic event had taken place there, nor, indeed, was it the last. It was there that God first promised the land of Canaan to Abraham. It was there that Jacob's well was to be discovered. It was by that very well that, wearied with His journey, Jesus sat and talked with the woman of Samaria, who went away cleansed of her sins. This beautiful place was often the scene of dramatic, soul-stirring events, but I question that there was any in all history so soul-stirring and moving as the one to which I call your attention now.

On either side of the valley of Shechem, two miles wide, stands a mountain—on the one side, Mount Ebal, rugged, barren, rocky; and on the other side, Mount Gerizim, wooded and beautiful. Any traveler to the land of Palestine today can tell you that you can stand on the top of Mount Ebal and talk with someone on the top of Mount Gerizim, almost without raising your voice, so perfect are the natural acoustics. The amphitheater provided by the valley is utterly natural and complete, and voices ring across it from peak to peak.

When the Israelites arrived at the foot of Mount Ebal they erected an altar, building it with stones on which no tool was used, so that the altar was undefiled by any handiwork of man. Plaster was put over it, and on the plaster was written the two tables of the law of God. For the first time since they had crossed Jordan the people's attention was drawn to an altar, the place of communion, the place of worship; and at the same time to the law of God written on it, the place of discipline, the place of obedience.

Then half of the people went up Mount Ebal and the

other half went up Mount Gerizim. On Mount Ebal were to be pronounced the sentence of judgment and the curse of disobedience. On Mount Gerizim were to be pronounced the blessing, the joy, and the glory that were to follow obedience and surrender to God. The tribes of Reuben, Gad, Asher, Zebulan, Dan, and Naphtali went up Mount Ebal, and two of them had already expressed their desire to retreat from Canaan. The price of possessing the land was too big, and, besides, they had left their families and herds on the other side of Jordan. On Mount Ebal they heard the curse that would follow disobedience. Trace the future history of Reuben and Gad—it is a story of disaster. Also take warning from their experience. Up Mount Gerizim went the tribes of Simeon, Levi, Judah, Issachar, Joseph, and Benjamin, to hear the promise of blessing that would follow obedience. Between these two mountains stood the Ark of the Covenant, indicating the presence of the Lord in the valley, with Joshua and the priests.

Joshua began to speak, his voice ringing throughout that wonderful amphitheater, and he pronounced to the people a curse and a blessing, life and death, heaven and hell. He pronounced the curse on disobedience, and related the blessings that would follow obedience, and the "Amen" of all the people on both mountains echoed across the valley. The united army stood, half on one mountain peak and half on the other, and assented to the verdict of God: if we disobey we shall die, but if we obey we shall live. If we turn from Him we shall perish; if we follow after Him we shall be blessed. What a scene, what a crowd, what an epoch-making moment!

But what significance has it for people today? Let me get to grips with this message as it challenges my own heart and yours. First of all, I would point out that the law of God was written at the foot of the mount of judgment. The fact that one is a Christian does not free him from the law of God. It is true that he is delivered from its sentence by virtue of the death of Another, but he is certainly not absolved from the obligation and responsibilities it imposes.

Listen to the Apostle Paul, the greatest preacher ever born, I would imagine: "There is therefore now no condemnation to them which are in Christ Jesus" (Rom. 8:1). Blessed truth! For the man who has repented, the man who has believed, the man who has accepted in his life the risen, triumphant Saviour, there is therefore now no condemnation. The sentence of the law has been passed upon his Substitute. That, my friends, is our position in the sight of heaven.

If you were to ask how it happened, Paul leaves us in no doubt. He says, "For the law of the Spirit of life in Christ Jesus hath made me free from the law of sin and death" (Rom. 8:2). What does he mean? Just this: that the moment a man fulfills God's demands, assents to His judgment, and believes on His Son, another law is put into operation in heaven. For God the Father has made a covenant that has been sealed with the blood of the Cross, a covenant with His Son that He would bestow the gift of life on all who repent and believe, and would give them the Holy Spirit to be a new principle of life within us. At the moment a man believes, he is baptized by the Spirit of God and indwelt by the Third Person of the Trinity. Therefore, "the law of the Spirit of life in Christ Jesus hath made me free from the law of sin and death."

In case any of us should doubt how that miracle takes place, Paul tells us that "what the law could not do, in that it was weak through the flesh"—what we cannot do of our-

selves because of our weakness and our sin and our failure—
"God sending his own Son in the likeness of sinful flesh, and
for sin, condemned sin in the flesh" (Romans 8:3).

Yes, there is a new principle now operating in the life of
him who has become a Christian. He has received resurrection life into his heart. He has been baptized by the Spirit of
God into the perfect, spotless, pure life of the holy Son of
God, who lived a perfect life and died an atoning death, and
ascended from the grave to the throne; who gives, not to a
few favorites, but to everybody, every man and woman who
has been born again, a new principle of life, the law of the
Spirit of life in Christ.

You ask why all this has been done? Listen to this: "That
the righteousness of the law might be fulfilled in us, who
walk not after the flesh, but after the Spirit" (Rom. 8:4).
The Christian has not finished with the law of God. He has
finished with its sentence, but he cannot avoid its standards.
And, in plain language, that means that holiness is not op-
tional. "Without holiness no man can see the Lord."

The whole trouble with many Christians today is that they
are only playing at being Christian. They have never really
gone in for a holy, dynamic Christian life, because they are
afraid to pay the price. I tremble in my own soul at the shock
many will get when they face our Lord and discover that
the beliefs they have cherished, the doctrines they have em-
braced, and the Bible they have said they believed, have
landed them in hell because their beliefs have never become
action, and the Bible has never become practice, and their
lives have never been made holy. The law at the foot of the
mount of judgment has to be fulfilled, not *by* us, thank
heaven, but *in* us by the Holy Spirit.

But let me point out something else—how thankful I am for this detail—the law was engraved on the altar. The altar was not placed in the beauty of Mount Gerizim, it was placed at the foot of the barrenness, and under the very sentence of judgment, on Mount Ebal, placed where man has been condemned.

Not one Christian can stand before God uncondemned by His law. There is not a single person redeemed by the blood of Jesus who can look into the face of God except to say, "I am free from condemnation and death, I am free from the sentence of the law; but, oh, God, how miserably I have failed to yield myself to the Holy Spirit, through whose power alone I can obey! And how tragically true it is that my Christian life has been a story of one breakdown after another, of failure, sin, unbelief, and I am ashamed of myself."

However, the law is written on the altar, and the altar was the place where the blood was shed, the place of communion, restoration, and worship. Therefore I am able to tell you, with such a thankful heart, that "if we walk in the light, as he is in the light," that if we come out from camouflage and sham and cherished tradition, and come right up before God and stand there conscious of our failure and sinfulness as Christians, if we dare to do that, then "we have fellowship one with another," He and us, "and the blood of Jesus Christ his Son cleanseth us from all sin" (I John 1:7). For "if we confess our sins, he is faithful and just to forgive us our sins, and to cleanse us from all unrighteousness" (I John 1:9).

Do you understand that the Christian is now facing the law and its demands on him? That the law is put before us, unrelenting in its standards, but a voice in my heart says, "If ye love me, keep my commandments" (John 14:15)? The

Christian is no longer facing the law as an obligation; he is facing it as a sheer delight to do the will of God, and from within him the love of God is shed abroad by the Holy Spirit. Because he is born from above, he hates what God hates and loves what God loves. He grieves and mourns over his sin for Jesus' sake more than for his own, and his heart's prayer is, "O God, make me holy." The child of God knows one constraining practice, devotion, and inspiration in his life; he is moved and compelled along because within him there is the fire of the love of Jesus.

> Jesus, Thine all-victorious love
>   Shed in my soul abroad;
> Then shall my heart no longer rove,
>   Rooted and fixed in God.
>
> Oh that in me the sacred fire
>   Might now begin to glow;
> Burn up the dross of base desire
>   And make the mountains flow.

The law is on the altar. Child of God, if you are convinced that you have broken it, if you are convinced that you have lost your passion, your zeal, and your devotion to the Lord Jesus, I beseech you to face the challenge of the law afresh and get back to the altar of communion. People come to me asking, "Should a Christian do this or that thing?" How absurd such questions are. How far must a Christian go in order to be saved? Only to the Cross. But if I am disobeying God in my life and cast off His law, it is an absolute declaration of the fact that within my heart I have abandoned worship at the Cross.

If you have no real heart longing for the Lord's work, no

real zeal for souls, and no real interest in His Word, it is because you have forsaken worship at Calvary. For when a man is dead to himself he has no problem with the things of the world or with what he should do or should not do. His cry is, "I delight to do thy will, O God," and "Oh, how I love thy law!"

As I conclude this chapter, may I ask you to observe that between the mountain of judgment and the mountain of blessing stood the Ark. There in the valley dividing the two was the presence of a holy God. It is utterly impossible for any of us to take up a neutral position. Faced by the challenge of God, some people get warm, some people get right with God, some people draw closer to Jesus, some people repent and humble themselves. But others drift away because the pace is too hot for them.

In heaven's name, I call on you to make your decision quickly, for the days are short. Do not sit under the ministry of the Word and trifle with God and play with New Testament holiness. The Church of the Lord Jesus Christ is not the place for you if you are not in earnest. We have too big a job to do, too big a challenge to face, for too soon the Lord will be here. Remember that Gideon got on better with three hundred than with thirty thousand men. In Jesus' name, I call on you, my dear worldly Christian, my dear man who is not right with God, to get to the Cross and get right with God.

There is no alternative. A man cannot be neutral—it is life or death. In this scene of Mount Gerizim and Mount Ebal I see a prophetic view of the day when Jesus shall come, and around Him shall be gathered all nations, and He shall separate them one from the other as the shepherd divides the sheep from the goats. One chooses life or death, blessing or cursing. In the name of my Lord Jesus, "I call heaven and earth to record this day against you, that I have set before you life and death, blessing and cursing: therefore choose life, that both thou and thy seed may live" (Deut. 30:19).

# CHAPTER 11

# ENEMY STRATEGY

## JOSHUA 9:3

*And when the inhabitants of Gibeon heard what Joshua had done unto Jericho and to Ai,*

*They did work wilily, and went and made as if they had been ambassadors, and took old sacks upon their asses, and wine bottles, old and rent, and bound up;*

*And old shoes and clouted upon their feet, and old garments upon them; and all the bread of their provision was dry and mouldy.*

*And they went to Joshua unto the camp of Gilgal, and said unto him, and to the men of Israel, We be come from a far country: now therefore make ye a league with us.*

*And the men of Israel said unto the Hivites, Peradventure ye dwell among us; and how shall we make a league with you?*

*And they said unto Joshua, We are thy servants. And Joshua said unto them, Who are ye? and from whence come ye?*

*And they said unto him, From a very far country thy servants are come because of the name of the Lord thy God: for we have heard the fame of him and all that he did in Egypt,*

*And all that he did to the two kings of the Amorites, that were beyond Jordan, to Sihon king of Heshbon, and to Og king of Bashan, which was at Ashtaroth.*

*Wherefore our elders and all the inhabitants of our country spake to us saying, Take victuals with you for the journey, and go to meet them, and say unto them, We are your servants: therefore now make ye a league with us.*

*This our bread we took hot for our provision out of our houses on the day we came forth to go unto you; but now, behold, it is dry, and it is mouldy:*

*And these bottles of wine, which we filled, were new; and, behold, they be rent: and these our garments and our shoes are become old by reason of the very long journey.*

*And the men took of their victuals and asked not counsel at the mouth of the Lord.*

*And Joshua made peace with them, and made a league with them, to let them live: and the princes of the congregation sware unto them.*

JOSHUA 9:3–15

All our constant struggles as Christians have one objective: full salvation and complete deliverance from sin. A battle won does not necessarily mean a victorious war. On the other hand, a battle lost does not mean that everything is hopeless. As long as sin lasts, conflict goes on. As long as you and I live in bodies whose redemption lies in the future, we shall know continually what it means to be tempted. No sin or evil is significant or can be treated lightly: to compromise with Satan is to court disaster.

The cause of defeat is always discovered by prayer but it takes more than prayer to recover ground we have lost. We do not subdue the enemy of our souls in a sudden moment of victory—the process of deliverance is gradual. Faith in, and obedience to, our great Commander-in-chief are the secrets of victorious living.

The law of God is given to the Christian, not to admire, but to obey. That law, fulfilled in the Christian's life by the indwelling of the Spirit of God, is the seal of the liberty in which we live. As we live in that liberty, we discover what it means to live victoriously.

These are some of the lessons that I trust we have been learning. Now let me remind you that the secret of winning a war lies in strategy. Notice how very carefully the war against the inhabitants of Canaan was planned by Joshua. He began by driving a wedge westward from Jericho right into the center of the land, thereby splitting the enemy opposition. Having done that, he wheeled south to destroy the southern foe, and finished mopping-up operations in the north later. It was a carefully planned campaign.

Now, the trouble with so many of us Christians is that we fail to apply divine strategy to daily living. If our Christian lives are hit-or-miss, it is not to be wondered at that we miss more than we hit! Very seldom does the Christian apply himself to daily disciplined action or to planned war against the enemy. The result is that many of us are completely outmaneuvered by Satan, who, if I may say so, is a master strategist. Remember, Satan is not only a roaring lion, he is also a subtle snake, and the roar of the lion is far less dangerous than the hiss of the snake.

In the ninth chapter of Joshua we come to a classic illustration of the subtlety of the enemy, of his wiles, and of our gullibility; but, thank heaven, also of the sovereignty of God, who overrules our mistakes for His glory. Let me ask you, therefore, to examine with me the wiliness of the enemy of our souls.

You will observe that the victories of the Israelites have called forth a concerted enemy attack. The first verse of this chapter implies that tribal warfare among the Canaanites has been put to one side. Petty squabbles have been forgotten; secondary issues have been submerged in an all-out effort to turn the tide against the invading army of Israel.

I must not allow myself to digress from the main objective here, but I must say this before I pass on: every victory that the Christian wins in his own personal life is an invitation for a full-scale attack by the enemy of his soul. Every time a child of God steps into an experience of blessing he is on the verge of another assault by the enemy. Our blessings and battles go side by side. If you are being pressed on every front and are in the thick of the fight, praise God! If you are finding temptation almost too much to bear and the struggle almost too hard to carry on, I want you to know that I am tremendously glad. You may be feeling miserable, but I am most thoroughly happy on your account. It is a good sign! If you are being tempted right and left it is because you are going right through with the will of God in blessing.

However, if you are saying to yourself, "I don't know what he is talking about; I haven't been tempted in years; I don't know anything about this kind of thing," do get before the Lord and ask Him to show you what is wrong with your life.

If only we—by we I mean the Christian Church—would lay aside every secondary issue to launch a full-scale attack on the enemy! The trouble is that we are too busy with our tribal warfare, too busy trying to settle our own petty squabbles, too busy splitting hairs about doctrinal matters (some of which, in the long run, will not matter very much), too busily engaged in seeking to deal with this question and that situation. There must be three cheers in hell because they have the Church of God bogged down with minor problems! If only we would learn that nothing less than a full-scale, united attack by all the people of God is the only hope for the Church of God in this twentieth century, Satan would find that he had stepped a bit too far and that we had learned from him.

But I want you to observe from this chapter that, before launching a full-scale attack on the Israelites, the inhabitants attempted to deceive the Israelites into making an alliance with them. After all, from the viewpoint of the Canaanites, a struggle did not hold out much hope for them. So far, the results had been all against them. Therefore, instead of launching a full-scale operation, a most subtle attempt is made to secure an alliance.

Let me refresh your memory. The Gibeonites arrived on the scene at Gilgal and pretended that they had traveled a very long way. They said they came from a particular region over which Joshua had no authority, concerning which God had given him no command whatsoever. In order to lend color to their story, they arrived with old shoes and garments that were worn and dirty, with wine bottles whose skins had been torn.

Furthermore, they were clever enough never to say a word about the defeats at Jericho and Ai. If they uttered a word about Jericho and Ai it would have been evident to the Israelites that they could not have come from very far. Otherwise how could they have heard that news? They referred only to what they had heard that the Israelites had accomplished on their journey through the wilderness. Not only so, but they asserted that they fully respected and honored and believed in the Israelites' God.

Satan is not going to like this—it will expose all his subtle ways. All that is absolutely typical of the devil! He knows full well that a Christian, a really committed Christian, is not going to be trapped by an open frontal attack. He knows that a child of God who has been seeking to go on with God and to get into blessing is on his guard. He is not going to be tripped up by an obvious attack.

So what does Satan do? He speaks to us concerning possible alliances that appear to be very trifling compared to our devotion to the Lord Jesus Christ. He speaks to us about a certain part of our lives over which, he suggests, the Lord Jesus Christ has no authority and concerning which Christ has given us no command, which is, as it were, so much on the circumference that it really will not matter anyway if we listen to the devil. He challenges us on the necessity for entire, thorough consecration. He speaks to us about the danger of "overdoing it." He warns us of the danger of becoming "too narrow." He will say, "Be careful that you don't get swept off your feet." He will claim at least a portion of our time and our money and our energy in order that, now and then at least, we can be lazy, and indulgent, or compromise. He will do everything that he can in order that, somehow or other, he may deceive us and cause us to lose the fine edge of our Christian witness. He is out to steal our affection, to lower our standard of Christian life, to cause us to compromise once in a while.

Are you aware of his tactics? I wonder if he has been trying this game on you, persuading you that you must take things a little more easily, that you must not go too far, that you must not overdo it. Is he seeking to suggest to you that there is at least some part of your life over which the sovereignty of Christ is unnecessary? Of course, remember that in all his talk he has glibly admitted his belief in God; he has always suggested that he himself is religious. Indeed, he has declared himself to be an absolute fundamentalist. The devil is all that: he is absolutely orthodox. Not for a moment would he disbelieve the Bible! Not for a moment would he disbelieve a Risen Lord and the fact of His coming again!

Because he has come to you in that disguise, he may easily have tripped you up. He has suggested to you, of course, that it is common sense which is needed in the business of the church. He has said to you that you must be very practical in the conduct of your affairs, especially regarding money. He has said to you that faith is irrational, that common sense is the thing which must always be practiced. Because he has come in such guise, Satan has been very difficult to detect. He has offered to help you with everything in his power, whereas, in point of fact, he is subtly accomplishing your ruin. "Believe not," says the Word of God, "every spirit, but try the spirits, whether they be of God" (I John 4:1).

It is far easier to deal with a Caiaphas than with a Judas, far easier to cope with an open enemy than with the subtlety of Satan's temptations. For the first time in the record of God's people there stood this day on holy ground in the camp at Gilgal a company of people who indeed were Israel's enemies. The Israelites, set apart for God, dedicated to Him, were mingled with those whom God had commanded them to destroy.

Alas, the tragedy that the Gibeonites have crept into church life and into personal Christian life, into Christian business life and into Christian home life! Satan has come in disguise and he is sapping away the very strength of our witness. Oh, the subtlety of the enemy!

But let me point out to you, also, the stupidity of the children of God. The language of verse 14 in this chapter is very ominous: "They asked not counsel of the mouth of the Lord."

It seems to take us a long time to learn the lesson that neglect of prayer always leads to trouble, and destroys the spirit of discernment. Neglect of prayer always suggests pride in our own judgment, which is fatal. Satan as an angel of light is so plausible. The foolish virgins so resembled those who were wise. The tares sown in the field are so similar to the wheat. The voice of the hireling sounds very like the voice of the shepherd. Bypath Meadow runs right alongside the King's Highway, and there is only a very narrow soft shoulder between the two.

Many an alliance that has brought ruin to a church and to a home, sadness and defeat to the Christian, has begun in exactly this way. How many through the years have come into church membership and have declared themselves to be utterly on the Lord's side, only in after years to have demonstrated by their lives that they never knew anything of the love of God or the victory of an indwelling Christ, and brought ruin, not support, to the testimony! How many church members there are whose lives are devoid of the love of Christ, who have no passion for souls, and who can go through life without caring that men go to hell, and therefore can never have been born again in Christ, in spite of all that they have said they believe!

How many a Christian has discovered that the things which seemed not to matter at the time have ruined his life! The power has been cut out of his Christian living because he has given Satan just one inch, has listened to his plausible words, and has yielded in some matter on the periphery of his life. Then the weakling finds that his testimony has been spoiled. How many have bought "just one copy" of a magazine that a Christian ought not to read and so have begun the downward path! How many have spent money on some luxury "just for once," and so have begun the downward road? How many a boy and girl have been trapped into a life partnership by the other's false cloak of Christianity!

> The perils that we well might shun
>    We saunter forth to meet;
> The path into the road of sin
>    We tread with careless feet.
> The air that comes instinct with death—
>    We bid it round us flow;
> And when our hands should bar the gate
>    We parley with the foe!

What is the answer? How can we ever match Satan and his subtle ways? Listen to me. Never, *never*, NEVER trust your own judgment in anything. When common sense says that a course is right, lift your heart to God, for the path of faith and the path of blessing may be in a direction completely opposite to that which you call common sense. When voices tell you that action is urgent, that something must be done immediately, refer everything to the tribunal of heaven. Then if you are still in doubt, dare to stand still. If you are called on to act and you have not time to pray, don't act. If you are called on to move in a certain direction and cannot wait until you have peace with God about it, don't move. Be strong enough and brave enough to dare to stand and wait on God, for none of them that wait on Him shall ever be ashamed. That is the only way to outmatch the devil.

Someone may answer, "All that you have been saying has gone like a sword into my heart. I have made my mistake; I have made my alliance in business; I have made my alliance in marriage, and as the years have gone by I have known what it means to suffer for it all. I can only pray that other people may be saved from what I have been going through. It is too late for me!"

Oh, no, my friend, that is the devil's lie! That is Satan's most subtle form of attack: get the Christian to make a blunder and then whisper into his ear, "I've got you tied."

Look at verse 21 in this chapter: "And the princes said unto them, Let them live; but let them be hewers of wood and drawers of water unto all the congregation." I think that is absolutely thrilling! I am so glad that, as I speak to you about the subtlety of Satan, I can tell you also that even for Satan's subtleties our God has the answer. We may make our mistakes, who doesn't? We may lose our battles—we all do. But listen to me, disheartened, discouraged Christian: the war can still be won. Thank God that He is able to overrule our sins and our mistakes, even to cause the curse to be turned into a blessing. These Gibeonites were made to hew wood and draw water for the house of the Lord. Isn't that wonderful? They were made to hew wood for the altar fire, to draw water for the cleansing ritual of the temple. The very thing in which the Israelites failed in this alliance and for which they suffered, they turned to a most wonderful account. Those who had deceived them were humiliated so much that they caused the altar flame to burn, and were used to purify the worship of God's people.

I want you to notice that there was no question of breaking the alliance with Gibeon. Indeed, future history reveals that the Israelites got into serious trouble when they tried to do so. Saul broke the league with the Gibeonites, and he suffered for it.

Fellow Christian, if you have made your mistake, lost your battle, and find yourself in difficulty, you cannot make that an excuse for breaking your word. The Christian is a man (or should be) of principle and integrity. Of course, mark you, there are some covenants better broken than kept. For example, Herod's oath to give anything she asked to the daughter of Herodias, who had inflamed him as she danced before him, was no justification for murder. For heaven's sake break today a covenant made in open, blatant sin.

But some Christian may have entered into a wrong alliance in business or in marriage, and find himself tied to a Gibeonite for the rest of his life. What about that? The Word is the answer, not me. "If any brother hath an unbelieving wife, and she is content to dwell with him, let him not leave her. . . . How knowest thou, O husband, whether thou shalt save thy wife?" (I Cor. 7:12, 16). Of course, young people, that cannot be taken as a reason for entering into marriage with an unbeliever, for if you do that, you are breaking the Word of God, which tells you not to be yoked with unbelievers.

If, however, you stepped into such a marriage inadvertently and found yourself linked in partnership with a man or woman who professed to be a Christian in order to win you, but since has made your life a hell on earth, the Word of God teaches very plainly that you cannot break that alliance. But the Word also tells you that if you come in humbleness of heart and acknowledge before God that you have sinned, He will cause the Gibeonite to whom you are married to be the chief means of bringing you to Him in prayer. The flame on the altar of your love for Jesus will burn the more brightly, and through your life many will be saved.

It happened to John Wesley. It has happened to many a man and many a woman since. What they thought was a curse, the mistake from which they thought they could never be free, which seemed to have ruined their testimony for right, was used by God to strengthen their prayer life and deepen their devotion. God turned the curse into a blessing!

Oh, the wonder of the love of God! Oh, the matchless grace of Jesus! Oh, the amazing providence of God which takes us, with all our mistakes, all our defeats, and all our sins, and overrules them all to His glory! He has looked into our face and we have looked into His, and we have said, "Lord, I'm sorry I have blundered. But, Lord, I believe you can restore the years that the cankerworm has eaten. I will refuse to allow the devil to drag me down and keep me down. I will forget the things which are behind and press on to those that are before."

I have discovered that the thing in which I have blundered, the sin that I have committed, the wrong that I have done, though the memory of it often haunts my life, is what now drives me daily to the Cross for cleansing, for forgiveness. for power. The wretched man who once was bound by sin discovers that the very sin which bound him is now the blessing which, more than anything else, brings him to consecrated service to his Saviour. What a wonderful Saviour we have!

# CHAPTER 12

# WINNING THROUGH

### JOSHUA 10:25

*Now it came to pass, when Adonizedec king of Jerusalem had heard how Joshua had taken Ai, and had utterly destroyed it; as he had done to Jericho and her king, so he had done to Ai and her king; and how the inhabitants of Gibeon had made peace with Israel, and were among them;*

*That they feared greatly, because Gibeon was a great city, as one of the royal cities, and because it was greater than Ai, and all the men thereof were mighty.*

*Wherefore Adonizedec king of Jerusalem sent unto Hoham king of Hebron, and unto Piram king of Jarmuth, and unto Japhia king of Lachish, and unto Debir king of Eglon, saying,*

*Come up unto me, and help me, that we may smite Gibeon: for it hath made peace with Joshua and with the children of Israel.*

*Therefore the five kings of the Amorites, the king of Jerusalem, the king of Hebron, the king of Jarmuth, the king of Lachish, the king of Eglon, gathered themselves together, and went up, they and all their hosts, and encamped before Gibeon, and made war against it.*

*And the men of Gibeon sent unto Joshua to the camp to Gilgal, saying, Slack not thy hand from thy servants; come up to us quickly, and save us, and help us: for all the kings of the Amorites that dwell in the mountains are gathered together against us.*

*So Joshua ascended from Gilgal, he, and all the people of war with him, and all the mighty men of valour.*

*And the Lord said unto Joshua, Fear them not: for I have delivered them into thine hand; there shall not a man of them stand before thee.*

*Joshua therefore came unto them suddenly, and went up from Gilgal all night.*

*And the Lord discomfited them before Israel, and slew them with a great slaughter at Gibeon, and chased them along the way that goeth up to Beth-horon, and smote them to Azekah, and unto Makkedah.*

*And it came to pass, as they fled from before Israel, and were in the going down to Beth-horon, that the Lord cast down great stones from heaven upon them unto Azekah, and they died: they were more which died with hailstones than they whom the children of Israel slew with the sword.*

*Then spake Joshua to the Lord in the day when the Lord delivered up the Amorites before the children of Israel, and he said in the sight of Israel, Sun, stand thou still upon Gibeon; and thou, Moon, in the valley of Ajalon.*

*And the sun stood still, and the moon stayed, until the people had avenged themselves upon their enemies. Is not this written in the book of Jasher? So the sun stood still in the midst of heaven, and hasted not to go down about a whole day.*

*And there was no day like that before it or after it, that* the Lord hearkened unto the voice of a man: for the Lord fought for Israel.

And Joshua returned, and all Israel with him, unto the camp to Gilgal.

But these five kings fled, and hid themselves in a cave at Makkedah.

And it was told Joshua, saying, The five kings are found hid in a cave at Makkedah.

And Joshua said, Roll great stones upon the mouth of the cave, and set men by it for to keep them.

And stay ye not, but pursue after your enemies, and smite the hindmost of them; suffer them not to enter into their cities: for the Lord your God hath delivered them into your hand.

And it came to pass, when Joshua and the children of Israel had made an end of slaying them with a very great slaughter, till they were consumed, that the rest which remained of them entered into fenced cities.

And all the people returned to the camp to Joshua at Makkedah in peace: none moved his tongue against any of the children of Israel.

Then said Joshua, Open the mouth of the cave, and bring out those five kings unto me out of the cave.

And they did so, and brought forth those five kings unto him out of the cave, the king of Jerusalem, the king of Hebron, the king of Jarmuth, the king of Lachish, and the king of Eglon.

And it came to pass, when they brought out those kings unto Joshua, that Joshua called for all the men of Israel, and said unto the captains of the men of war which went with him, Come near, put your feet upon the necks of them.

And Joshua said unto them, Fear not, nor be dismayed, be

*strong and of good courage: for thus shall the Lord do to all
your enemies against whom ye fight.*

*And afterward Joshua smote them, and slew them, and
hanged them on five trees: and they were hanging upon the
trees until the evening.*

JOSHUA 10: 1–26

Strange paradox as it may seem to some, nevertheless it is
eternally true that the land of full blessing is a land of intensive warfare. We have to learn to conquer and then we have
to learn to possess all that is ours in a Risen Lord.

We have studied the entry into the land of Canaan,
picturing the entry into the fullness of blessing, and I have
reminded you that the conquest of the land was the result of
three specific campaigns, in each of which there were decisive battles. First, there was the central campaign, in which
Joshua and his armies split the opposition and prevented a
united counter-attack. Then there was the southern campaign, in which the enemy was defeated, and finally, the
northward sweep, in which the plan of invasion was accomplished. All this, please note, was according to carefully prepared design and strategy.

Satan's attacks on the child of God are always carefully
planned. An outstanding example is his frontal attack on
our Lord in the wilderness. Our counter-attacks on the devil
seldom are based on any strategy at all. Too often we trust to
half-hearted and hot-headed methods, which end in defeat
and tragedy for us.

In the central campaign, the decisive battles were Jericho
and Ai. In the southern campaign they were at Gibeon and
Beth-horon (Joshua 10), and in the northern campaign by
the waters of Merom (Joshua 11). Probably there were

many other battles, but those I have mentioned decided the course of these particular campaigns.

I have reminded you that the loss of one battle in the Christian life does not necessarily mean ultimate defeat. But I want to emphasize that what we do at critical junctures may well prove to be decisive in a wide area of Christian experience.

Now we have considered the first part of Joshua's campaign, the slash through the center of Canaan. We have learned, I trust, important lessons—that disobedience and prayerlessness mean inevitable defeat, while obedience, constant watchfulness, and utter reliance on the Lord insure victory. Learn those lessons, my dear young Christians, at an early point in your experience, and you will make a good beginning, which is very vital in every aspect of life.

But let us turn to the southern sweep of Joshua's campaign, recorded in chapter 10, and we shall find that new situations and new dangers are matched by faith, action, and ruthless, uncompromising, daring warfare, which resulted in total victory.

Let me briefly recount the story of this somewhat long chapter. Five Canaanite kings have become very scared by the alliance Joshua has made with the Gibeonites. Therefore they unite together to declare war on Gibeon, who immediately sent a call for help to their new ally, Joshua. Assured of God's promise of victory, Joshua came up from Gilgal, his base of operations, and defeated and chased the enemy. Then followed one of the greatest battles of all history, in which God deliberately intervened on the behalf of His people. He delayed nightfall and lengthened the day in order that victory should be utterly complete and final. The five kings were then captured and imprisoned.

When the battle was over, Joshua commanded his captains to bring the kings out of their hiding place and instructed his leaders to put their feet upon the captives' necks, a most humiliating experience for the enemy kings. Then Joshua, facing his army, seems to have caught fire. "And Joshua said unto them, Fear not, nor be dismayed, be strong and of good courage: for thus shall the Lord do to all your enemies against whom ye fight" (10:25). One would almost think that this would have been sufficient, but not content with this gesture of contempt, Joshua slew the five kings and hung the body of each on a tree. Cruel Joshua! Do you think so?

The result of this battle is graphically described in verse 21, which tells us "that none moved his tongue against any of the children of Israel." From that time onward the people of God were finally established in the land of Canaan as a people to be feared. This sweeping victory proved that Jericho and Ai were no mere chance. Such a victory demonstrated that the Israelites were no ordinary people, that this strange nation which had come up from Egypt, through the wilderness, through the Jordan, and had conquered the impregnable Jericho, were indeed supported by supernatural power, and were to be feared.

I believe with all my heart that God's purpose for His church today is the same—to make it a church to be feared. Speaking of the church for a moment in terms of a building, it should be a place to which people almost fear to come lest they be converted. A church as a fellowship should be composed of people who are uncompromising in their testimony, courageous in their faith, and holy in their lives. In the church services there should be the awe and reverence demanded by the presence of God.

This is God's purpose not only for His church, but also for every truly regenerate man or woman of God—that they shall be feared. The Christian man is he who is righteous in his conduct, uncompromising in his principles, passionate in his devotion to his Saviour, sacrificial in his service, and transparent in his life. He has no life behind the scenes to which he retreats to indulge his appetite for things that he would be ashamed to do in the company of Christian people. His life will bear the closest scrutiny of his strongest critics, from which he will come out unscathed, a holy man of God continually."

If this be the purpose of God, and I question that anyone could argue the point in the light of God's plan of redemption through the blood of Jesus Christ, let us ask ourselves how it can be true for us and for our churches. Oh to have the awe of God in the hearts of the people and the preacher! Oh that when people come to church on Sunday there might be something about the place that would speak to them of heaven!

How can we achieve this? Notice quite clearly in the book of Joshua that there was no battle at all until Joshua took the initiative, and started to attack. The Lord Jesus once said that the gates of hell shall not prevail against His church; He never suggested that the gates of hell would suddenly somehow become uprooted and begin to march toward God's people on earth. What He said was rather that the gates of hell would never be able to stand against the onslaught of a Spirit-filled company of His people. In the light of His Word, it is God's plan that His people should always be on the offensive, never on the defensive. Too often we retreat, run away, hide from the devil, instead of launching a full scale offensive in the name of Jesus

I think the answer to the questions we ask concerning this victorious faith is found in a study of the plight of the five kings at the place called Beth-horon. Let me ask you to observe them in three circumstances.

First of all, in the 17th verse of this chapter we are told that they hid in a cave. We would ask how they came to hide themselves. They had great armies and great power. How was Joshua so successful in making them hide from him in fear? If you take time to read this chapter through for yourselves, you will find that one word occurs five times, and it is the key to victory. The word is "Gilgal."

Joshua came up from Gilgal to meet the enemy. He was at that place again half way through, and at the end of the battle, when victory was won, he went there again. All through this campaign, from beginning to end, he kept open the lines of communication with Gilgal. I do trust that the lessons of Gilgal have been as well learned by us.

May I remind you of the great words of New Testament truth and salvation which have their roots deeply imbedded in Gilgal. Here they are; refresh your memory. It was a place of *remembrance*, where all of God's people together went down unto death; it was a place of *resurrection*, where together they came up with their leader into life. It was a place of *renunciation*, where they cast off the carnal existence of the wilderness; it was a place of *restoration*, where they came again into fellowship with the Lord. It was the place of *realization*, where they began to taste of the strong food of the land; it was the place of *revelation*, where they met their Captain with a drawn sword.

The Christian life has its roots firmly imbedded in Calvary, the place where we died with Jesus and rose with Him, where we have deliberately renounced carnality and have entered into a living fellowship with our Lord, where we have begun to take the strong food of His Word and to realize every moment of our lives that the Captain of the Lord's hosts is with us.

Gilgal is not merely a surrender at the very beginning, but an attitude maintained throughout the campaign. Therefore the secret of this sweeping conquest at Beth-horon was first of all in these words—an attitude maintained.

Is the line of communication between your life and the throne in heaven open today? There will be no victory until it is. Can you look up into the face of our Lord and know that His smile is on you? Perhaps you thought that surrender to Him is accomplished in a single act. I say that it is not an act but a permanent attitude, in which lies the only secret of power.

Observe here, in the second place, the kings in an even more humiliating position. Verse 24 tells us that they were forced to lie full length on the ground, and that five of Joshua's captains were ordered to stand on the captives' necks. Why should they be so publicly humiliated? I'll tell you why: they were humiliated before all God's people in order that the whole army of Israel might know that it was the Lord who had wrought the victory. "Thus shall the Lord do to all your enemies."

My beloved friends, the Lord Jesus Christ fought for you and me at Calvary and won. No part of your life, no deeply rooted sin or habit or weakness, but comes within the scope of the cleansing, delivering power of His blood. His salvation is an all-inclusive salvation for you. The Lord God has fought for you, my friends, and, praise God, He has won.

But it was not only that they might know that the Lord had won the victory for them. It was also—please mark this carefully—in order to show to the Israelites that the victory God had won for them had to be personally appropriated. "Thus shall the Lord do to all your enemies *against whom ye fight*."

You may say to me, "But the Christian life is not a life of fighting, it is a life of faith." Are you quite sure about that? Surrender to Christ is not enough. Our consecration to the Lordship of Christ is not enough. There will be no victory in the name of Christ until you declare total war against everything in your life that is sinful. Fancy you and me having our feet on the neck of jealousy, of pride, of a critical spirit, of a harsh tongue! Fancy our having our feet on the neck of every crippling thing in our Christian testimony!

Every gain I have made in Christian character will be resisted by the devil down to the end of life's journey, and there will be no personal experience of the power of Jesus Christ in victory until I declare war on sin. I ask you in the name of heaven, are you attacking on all fronts? Have you identified yourselves by declaring war on pride, on self, on tongue, and on criticism, by determining to attack and conquer them in the name of Jesus? You have a constant attitude to maintain, and a victory to claim.

The third thing I want to point out from this story is another extraordinary situation, five kings hanging on five trees. Wasn't that a bit rough? Poor fellows, they had been hiding in a cave, and then they had been pulled out, and forced to lie on the ground and have Joshua's captains put their feet on their necks. That would be enough for one day. Send them back into the cave and let them stay there—they will be all right; they will be too scared to come out again. Cruel Joshua!

I remind you again of something I said before: that God's purpose for this land was Bethlehem, Calvary, and Pentecost, and the iniquity of the inhabitants of the land was full. Nothing must be allowed to stand in the way of the complete purpose of God for victory—everything must be wiped out. It was not enough to leave five kings lurking in a cave—they must be slain.

Oh, how I have been praying that the Holy Spirit might write this most important truth on your hearts! This is not consecration; what I am talking about, fellow Christians, is sanctification. In each one of us is an old nature, a self which is incapable of holiness, which has been judged and condemned to die at the Cross. There is also in each one of us a new nature, which is incapable of sin, which has been imparted to us by faith in Jesus Christ our Lord. But it is only insofar as I am prepared to submit to the wounds, to the nails, to the crucifixion of self, that I can enjoy the victory of Christ. I dare not leave sin lurking within the hidden recesses of my heart still unjudged.

You are glad that you are a forgiven sinner? You are glad that you are covered by the blood of Jesus and are on the road to heaven? So am I. You are glad to know that there is, therefore, now no condemnation to you that are in Christ Jesus? You are glad for all that, and you are singing the songs of Zion, *but* in your life may be sin which has never been brought out, confessed, forsaken, judged and condemned by you. And you wonder why your testimony isn't radiant, why your witness isn't effective!

It may be because lurking within you is a tongue which is desperately critical about other people—a tongue that has never been put to death, or a pride that has never been crucified, or a lust that has never been confessed to God. Perhaps a selfish desire for self-glorification is alive in the cave inside your body. Oh, yes, it is forgiven; oh, yes, it is under the blood; yes, there is no condemnation—hallelujah for all that! But you know from your own experience that, from time to time, the thing inside that cave will suddenly dash out, and before you realize what has happened, you will have been unkind and unjust, critical and bad-tempered. Satan has come out of his hiding place and got you.

There is one royal road to victory: an attitude of constancy to maintain, a victory to claim, *and* a danger to shun. Take shelter under the blood of the Cross and make your hiding place in the wounds of Jesus; never take sides with sin, but declare total war on the serpent that lurks in your own heart. How may that serpent be slain? Jesus slew it for you.

Some Christian who would step into a real experience of triumph, into an attacking faith, will determine no longer to be bogged down by the years that have gone, but to enter into a victorious experience. This is what he will do: he will go to some brother or some sister whom he has wronged desperately, and apologize. He will fall at the Master's feet, and confess the whole story to Him. He will thank the Lord Jesus that it was all dealt with at Calvary! He will thank Him that even late in life he is able to gain victory over his selfishness, and his tongue, and his criticism, and his judgment, and all the rest.

And then what will he do? He will look up into the face of the living Lord and put his feet by faith on the enemy, and he will say, "Thus shall the Lord do to all my enemies against whom I fight." Then for the first time in his life he will go out attacking on all fronts, declaring total war in his soul against everything that has not yet been judged, condemned, and confessed before God.

> Fight the good fight with all thy might;
> Christ is thy strength and Christ thy right;
> Lay hold of life, and it shall be
> Thy joy and crown eternally.

# CHAPTER 13

# THE FRUIT OF VICTORY
### JOSHUA 11:23

*As the Lord commanded Moses his servant, so did Moses command Joshua, and so did Joshua; he left nothing undone of all that the Lord commanded Moses.*

*So Joshua took all that land, the hills, and all the south country, and all the land of Goshen, and the valley, and the plain, and the mountain of Israel, and the valley of the same;*

*Even from the mount Halak, that goeth up to Seir, even unto Baalgad in the valley of Lebanon under mount Hermon: and all their kings he took, and smote them, and slew them.*

*Joshua made war a long time with all those kings.*

*There was not a city that made peace with the children of Israel, save the Hivites the inhabitants of Gibeon: all other they took in battle.*

*For it was of the Lord to harden their hearts, that they should come against Israel in battle, that he might destroy them utterly, and that they might have no favour, but that he might destroy them, as the Lord commanded Moses.*

*And at that time came Joshua, and cut off the Anakims from the mountains, from Hebron, from Debir, from Anab.*

*and from all the mountains of Judah, and from all the mountains of Israel: Joshua destroyed them utterly with their cities.*

*There was none of the Anakims left in the land of the children of Israel: only in Gaza, in Gath, and in Ashdod, there remained.*

*So Joshua took the whole land, according to all that the Lord said unto Moses; and Joshua gave it for an inheritance unto Israel according to their divisions by their tribes. And the land rested from war.*

JOSHUA 11:15–23

Chapter 11 of the book of Joshua marks the point at which united action in Canaan by the people of God ceases. Their victories have been decisive, and though the enemy still lived in Canaan, nevertheless they were beaten and scattered. God had given the whole land to His people.

Much territory was yet to be possessed, but it was left to each tribe to possess what potentially it had received through the conquest of the whole people in which it had taken part. Each tribe was to apply individually the lessons it had learned in united war if it was to possess its inheritance. That the tribes failed to do so was not a reflection on the power of God, but on their failure to take for themselves what Joshua had given and allotted to each one of them.

I would pause to say what is tremendously important (I don't know how many realize it), that every precious truth we learn must be applied by faith and appropriated individually into our personal lives, or else it will mean nothing whatsoever. The blessing and the glow and the warmth that we receive in our hearts can be dissipated ten minutes after we close this book. He who is to go on with God in this pilgrim journey and walk with Christ in victory and in power until he meets his Lord face to face, will seek a quiet place where he can reflect on what God has said to him, where he can thank the Lord for the truth he has received, and where he may claim for himself personally what God in Jesus Christ has done for all His church as a body.

It is true that the victory of the Cross was decisive, but it is also true that one will experience only as much of that victory as by faith he appropriates personally. May God give His church in these days people who are desperate to be right with Him and utterly dissatisfied with what they are apart from His grace.

I want to show you what is the fruit of victory. You will find it in Joshua 11:23, "Joshua took the whole land, according to all that the Lord said unto Moses, and Joshua gave it for an inheritance unto Israel according to their divisions by their tribes, and the land rested from war." "Joshua took the whole land"—victory was complete. "Joshua gave it for an inheritance" to the people; whether they received it or not depended on their individual faith to go into it and possess it. "And the land rested from war."

The greatest source of conflict in Christian life is in not being right with God, in permitting in one's life that which he knows to be contrary to the will of God. Such a one is at war with heaven. The moment he begins to obey, immediately his soul rests from war.

Let us look first at the fruit of victory in the life of the Lord Jesus Himself. "The land rested from war." United action is over, victory has been won. All this is in keeping with the spiritual analogy we are tracing through this book of Joshua. I am certain that we are not following cunningly devised fables, but are tracing the spiritual teaching that runs right through the Word of God and which can satisfy every need. The conquest, apportionment, and victory of Canaan is but an Old Testament analogy of the resurrection and ascension of Jesus Christ to the throne in heaven. As the writer to the Hebrews says concerning Him, "Who . . . when he had by himself purged our sins, sat down on the right hand of the Majesty on high" (Heb. 1:3).

Throughout the whole book of Joshua we have seen that the land of Canaan corresponds in the New Testament to our inheritance in Jesus Christ. What the land was to Israel, Christ is to you and me. The land rested from war: Jesus sat down at the right hand of the Majesty on high—the victory was won. He has taken the whole territory, and there is no part of the dominion of hell, whether it be in the world or in heavenly places, which the victory of the cross has not finally overthrown. Throughout the whole created universe Jesus Christ is Lord because of Calvary.

All the power of materialistic Communism sweeping through this world cannot move an inch except by the permission of Jesus Christ. He is Master. Oh, my fellow Christians, what a hallelujah it should bring to your hearts to know that you are on the victory side! Having won the victory, Jesus has ascended into heaven to give to every one of God's believing children who is prepared by faith to take it, his portion of the victory of the Cross. "When He had by Himself purged our sins, He sat down." Majestic rest!

I want you to think just for a moment with me about "the rest" of the Lord Jesus. What kind of rest is it? It is certainly not the rest of exhaustion. When you and I sit down it is usually because we are tired. The Lord Jesus never spared Himself; His was a life of unceasing toil, unsleeping vigil, bitter sorrow, the anguish of Gethsemane, the burden of human sin. But none of these things exhausted Him. Neither is it the rest of inactivity, for the concluding verses of the Gospel of Mark tell us that the disciples "went forth, and preached everywhere, the Lord working with them, and confirming the word with signs following" (Mark 16:20).

His is surely the rest of satisfaction. Had He not left His throne, stripped Himself of His glory, and made an end of sin by offering up Himself? Did He not cry out, "It is finished"? Now, neither weary nor inactive, but satisfied, our precious Lord sits in absolute assurance, in complete and calm expectation, that one day the fruits of the Cross will be reaped. Nothing can be added to the finished work of salvation. Our Lord sits in heavenly places today because the sacrifice of the Cross has been demonstrated to be sufficient and complete for the salvation of the world. "He has," says Hebrews 10:12, "offered one sacrifice for sins for ever." The demands of God's justice have been satisfied, the sword of God's justice has been sheathed, and today there is now no condemnation to those who believe in Jesus Christ and follow Him.

The rest of the Saviour is the rest of calm, the rest of poise, the rest of assurance, the rest of satisfaction, the rest from work that has been completed; all that need be done for the salvation of every soul has been accomplished, and therefore He has sat down.

We must realize that as the Lord Jesus is there, He wears our nature. He is there as a man, for His fellow men, and it is God's purpose that you and I should share that rest with Him. Such was the thought in the mind of the Apostle Paul in Ephesians 2:6, that He has "made us sit together in heavenly places in Christ Jesus."

My dear Christian friends, I want you to understand that

the very heart of our salvation, the real thrill and joy of Christian experience is this: that in reference to His death, His resurrection, and His ascension, it is always "together with Christ." Because of that, Jesus desires that you and I should enter into that rest in terms of the experience of daily life. The fruit of victory for Christ is rest. The fruit of entering into our share in that victory in Christ is exactly the same—rest.

What is the effect of that rest in Christian life today? You cannot get the highest result from your work if you are always rushing at fever heat. The work of God can never be done effectively until we learn to rest in His strength that He may mold us, until we learn to let the fever, the rush, the worry, and the excitement subside into the rest of Jesus.

A year or two ago I was showing a friend in London around St. Paul's Cathedral. Much to my dismay, he desired to go right up to the top, and there are almost four hundred steps! He was an international football player, a very fine Christian man, and he made me very conscious of advancing weight! In fact, he arrived at the top by the time I had made about half of the steps. When eventually I caught him up, breathless and excited, at the very turret of the great Cathedral, I noticed that it was a brilliant September day. (We have such days occasionally in London.) The sun was shining out of a clear blue sky on the golden cross above us on the dome. We could look up to see it shining with brilliant loveliness in that beautiful sky, but when we looked down we could see nothing! London was lost in fog, smoke, and dirt. To me that was a picture of the Christian life. It is the purpose of God in Jesus Christ to lift us every day of our lives above the grime and fog and conflict of daily living into the clear blue sky of the love of heaven and of the rest of Jesus. I wonder if you and I are enjoying that love and rest.

The restful Christian is he who lives His life above the storm with Jesus. Oh, he is sensitive to sorrow and to the troubles of other people, but he is able always to discern the wisdom of God. He is willing to trust the loving heart of God and therefore is able in the conflict to await the unfolding of God's plan. He is able to keep silent while he waits on the Word of God. The Christian who is living there, above the toil and traffic of daily life, who is constantly living in touch with the throne, is resting in Jesus. He is also the busiest man of all, going at such a speed you wonder that he doesn't break down. The only answer he can give you is that as he has waited on the Lord he has exchanged his puny strength for the almighty energy of the Holy Spirit. The resting Christian—are you like that? I didn't say the lazy Christian, I said the *resting* Christian: busy, keen, always at the work of the Master, while deep in his heart is peace that no storm, however unexpected, and no sorrow, however miserable and hard to bear, can ever disturb.

How can that rest be yours and mine? Surely you would covet it for yourself, as I do constantly for my own heart and life. First of all, it is the rest of assured forgiveness. You see, he who is resting in the Lord Jesus like this is no longer working toward the Cross to obtain forgiveness—he is at the foot of the Cross sharing its victory, he sees the sunshine of heaven blazing down on it, and he knows that Christ has done all that needs to be done to save him. He has heard the cry, "It is finished!" He listens to the Word of God—"Who shall lay anything to the charge of God's elect?" (Rom. 8:33). That man knows that he was together with Jesus in death, and the judgment of his sin is finished. He stands before God, in spite of the consciousness of his own imperfection, clothed with all the righteousness and beauty of his precious Saviour. He is living above the dirt and fog because he is resting in what Jesus is.

Are you always worrying about your past sin, always wanting to drag it up and talk about it with somebody, always letting it disturb you, always wanting to discuss it with folks, to confess it to others? Beloved, may I say that what God has put under the blood, God has forgotten; you forget it too, and rest in the work of Calvary.

This rest of the Christian life is not only the rest of forgiveness, but also the rest of victory. Oh, how often we have sought to oppose Satan in our own strength and by our own resolve! We have fought and we have struggled, then have started all over again and failed again. But when the child of God begins to see that Christ has done everything and to understand that Satan is a conquered foe, he finds the rest of victory. He begins to realize that the devil cannot touch the life of the child of God who is resting in Jesus, for his life is hid with Christ in God. Then the child of God understands indeed that he is one with Christ in death and one with Him in resurrection.

There is nothing—no circumstance, no trouble, no testing —that can ever touch me until, first of all, it has gone past God and past Christ, right through to me. If it has come that far, it has come with a great purpose, which I may not understand at the moment; but as I refuse to become panicky, as I lift my eyes up to Him and accept it as coming from the throne of God for some great purpose of blessing to my own heart, no sorrow will ever disturb me, no trial will ever disarm me, no circumstance will cause me to fret, for I shall rest in the joy of what my Lord is. That is the rest of victory.

Added to all this, the Christian who is resting in the Lord is calm in every situation, and divine strength to work is given him. There is something about him, or about her, that conveys the impression of spiritual efficiency and dynamic because the power of God is there in place of his own puny strength. It is operating because he is resting in assured forgiveness, in victory, and, above all, because he has surrendered his will to the will of God.

My friends, I wonder how many of us can really say today that his will is no longer the tool of selfish desire but is being used of the Holy Spirit. It is then that a Christian begins to work in harmony with all the purposes of God. When our will is surrendered to God and all its action flows from the power plant of God's will, then disappointment becomes His appointment, and life is no longer a ceaseless struggle to try to get Him to do something that we think He ought to do. Then, in the desire to do God's will, prayer becomes unbroken fellowship and unclouded communion.

There is a verse in the Bible which I had found very hard to believe; it is only recently that I have really grasped it, and since then I have often passed it on to other people. It is Psalm 37:4, which says, "Delight thyself in the Lord; and he shall give thee the desires of thine heart."

"Some desires, Lord?"

"No, my child, all desires, every one of them."

"But there must be some exceptions."

"No, there is not one exception. Delight thyself in the Lord."

Subdue your will to the will of God, and He will give you every desire of your heart. Why? Because he whose life is lived on the principle of a surrendered will desires only the will of God in everything. All is ours when we discover that not only are we together with Christ in death and resurrection, but also together with Him in rest.

I am so glad that God does not make the way into full salvation difficult and complicated, because some of us would never get there. Perhaps it is the simplicity of it that disarms us. Let me ask you this: do you desire this life of rest in Jesus —the rest of assured forgiveness, the rest of unbroken fellowship, the rest of a surrendered will, the rest of a life which is satisfied in Him? Has your Christian life been so much a battle of frustrated desires and unsatisfied longings? How may you have a life of rest? Read this verse again: "Joshua took the whole land, and Joshua gave it for an inheritance . . . and the land had rest from war."

Our Joshua, the Lord Jesus, has taken the whole land. All the fruit of Calvary is at the disposal of every one of His children, and He holds out in His arms the whole of it to give it to you as your inheritance. It is what Peter referred to on the day of Pentecost, when he said, ". . . having received of the Father the promise of the Holy Spirit, he hath shed forth this." All that is asked of you and me if we would enter into the land of full salvation and rest in Jesus Christ is that we should take our share of the victory of the Cross.

If I always look within myself for this rest, what happens? I will start looking for an unscriptural experience of the Holy Spirit and I will think I am not saved because I haven't what some people call "the real baptism" and because I cannot speak in tongues. If I look within, I will become fanatical. If I look without and up to Christ without reckoning on the presence of the Spirit of God, I shall look in despair and say He is too far away, the prospect is too high, and I can never reach it. But if I look up to the Cross in the clearness of God's blue sky and know that it is empty because He who was crucified on it is sitting at God's right hand holding out all the inheritance of life and blessing for me—if at the same time I believe that He has shed into my heart the Holy Spirit to make it all real down here, then my soul will rest from war. I shall live above the noise, the clamor, the rush—above the dirt and the sin. I shall be resting in Christ, thankful that He has sent me the Holy Spirit to make His presence real to me.

# CHAPTER 14

## POSSESSING OUR POSSESSIONS

### JOSHUA 13:1

*Now these are the kings of the land, which the children of Israel smote, and possessed their land on the other side Jordan toward the rising of the sun, from the river Arnon unto mount Hermon, and all the plain on the east:*

*Sihon king of the Amorites, who dwelt in Heshbon, and ruled from Aroer, which is upon the bank of the river Arnon, and from the middle of the river, and from half Gilead, even unto the river Jabbok, which is the border of the children of Ammon;*

*And from the plain to the sea of Chinneroth on the east, and unto the sea of the plain, even the salt sea on the east, the way to Bethjeshimoth; and from the south, under Ashdoth-pisgah:*

*And the coast of Og king of Bashan, which was of the remnant of the giants, that dwelt at Ashtaroth and at Edrei,*

*And reigned in mount Hermon, and in Salcah, and in all Bashan, unto the border of the Geshurites and the Maachathites, and half Gilead, the border of Sihon king of Heshbon.*

*Them did Moses the servant of the Lord and the children of Israel smite: and Moses the servant of the Lord gave it for a possession unto the Reubenites, and the Gadites, and the half tribe of Manasseh.*

JOSHUA 12:1–6

*Now Joshua was old and stricken in years; and the Lord said unto him, Thou art old and stricken in years, and there remaineth yet very much land to be possessed.*

*This is the land that yet remaineth: all the borders of the Philistines, and all Geshuri,*

*From Sihor, which is before Egypt, even unto the borders of Ekron northward, which is counted to the Canaanite: five lords of the Philistines; the Gazathites, and the Ashdothites, the Eshkalonites, the Gittites, and the Ekronites; also the Avites:*

*From the south, all the land of the Canaanites, and Mearah that is beside the Sidonians, unto Aphek, to the borders of the Amorites:*

*And the land of the Giblites, and all Lebanon, toward the sunrising, from Baalgad under mount Hermon unto the entering into Hamath.*

*All the inhabitants of the hill country from Lebanon unto Misrephothmaim, and all the Sidonians, them will I drive out from before the children of Israel: only divide thou it by lot unto the Israelites for an inheritance, as I have commanded thee.*

JOSHUA 13:1–6

A casual reader of the book of Joshua might be tempted to pass over chapters 12 and 13 very hurriedly, for to a cursory reading they contain merely the record of territories in Canaan, a list of names and places, some of which are hard to pronounce and harder still to understand. If, however, you yielded to that temptation you would miss a very great deal. The greatest treasures of God's Word are not lying on the surface for us lightly and easily to pick up.

We are therefore going to consider briefly this 12th chapter, which summarizes the extent of the conquest so far in Canaan. The first six verses tell us of conquests under Moses' leadership; verses 7 to 24 tell us of the conquest under the leadership of Joshua.

The conquests under Moses, of course, referred to battles in the wilderness, on the east side of Jordan. The conquests under Joshua covered the battles in the land itself. Under Moses, certain territory had become the inheritance of Reuben, Gad, and half the tribe of Manasseh, according to their own expressed desire. We are informed in this chapter of just the degree to which Joshua and his armies conquered part of the land of Canaan. There follows a list of thirty-one powerful kings who had occupied certain territory in the land, but all of whom are now subdued and submissive to the people of God.

Sometimes in the course of human experience it is good to sit down and reflect on what has been conquered by the grace of God. Not boastfully, but with a humble and grateful heart, to survey the years that have gone and to go over the pages of memory carefully to recall where the grace of God has triumphed, so that we will be able to look into His face and say, "But where sin abounded, grace did much more abound" (Rom. 5:20).

For some people, most of the battles of life are over; they have few left to fight. To many others, however, most of life's battles are yet to be fought. Whether they have been fought or are yet to come, may God grant to us all to be able to say when the journey ends, "I have fought a good fight, I have finished my course, I have kept the faith" (II Tim. 4:7).

Before we leave this chapter altogether, I would refer you to the sixth verse, which tells us that "Moses, the servant of the Lord, gave it [the land conquered by Moses] for a possession." These words are nearly the same as those in chapter 11:23, if we substitute the name "Moses" for the name "Joshua." But oh, what a difference there is!

I must not press Scripture analogy too far, though I think I am justified in employing it to illustrate a doctrine which is well-established in other parts of God's Word. These two and a half tribes which Moses settled beyond Jordan took little part in the national life of Israel and soon completely lost their inheritance. They appear to have been absorbed by the nations which they were supposed to overcome. They had chosen the eastern side, the wilderness side of the land.

The lesson I want to write deeply on your hearts, in passing, is this: that whatever Moses, the representative of the law, gives to any of us must ultimately slip through our fingers, that we must inevitably fail in all that we try to be in the power of our own resolution. The deepest blessings of the spiritual life cannot be held in the strength of our own purpose. They can be ours only in fellowship with the Lord Jesus Christ, in whom all our inheritance is vested, and from whom we receive every blessing by faith. For "God . . . hath blessed us with all spiritual blessings in heavenly places in Christ" (Eph. 1:3). Would to God that we would learn that lesson and cease attempting to reach the land of blessing by our own effort alone!

We will now consider more especially Joshua 13:1, in which we read, "Now Joshua was old and stricken in years; and the Lord said unto him, Thou art old, and stricken in years, and there remaineth yet very much land to be possessed." Joshua was about ninety years old, and much of the land was still unsubdued and remained to be possessed.

The first six verses of this chapter give us a very clear demarkation of the unpossessed territory. There must be no resting on past achievements, otherwise God's purpose for Israel could never be realized. As the opening verses of the book of Joshua told us, God had given the Israelites, in intention, all of the land, but they must possess every inch of the inheritance themselves. The method of setting about possessing this land, which occupies the remainder of the book of Joshua, was, first of all, to survey it, then to apportion it among the several tribes, and last, to leave each tribe to appropriate that which was given to it. I hope you understand clearly that principle, for we shall be looking at it again.

It would be interesting to examine the extent of the area of the land designated by the Holy Spirit as an inheritance for the chosen people. It extended from the region of Philistia in the north to the rich pasture lands in the south. Were we to compare what God intended them to have with the land which the Israelites actually possessed and held, we would notice an appalling difference between the two. Never in all their history did the Israelites achieve God's intention.

Now I must leave the record of history to apply the spiritual lesson of it to our own lives. In the Lord Jesus Christ is set forth the heavenly inheritance which God purposes that each of us should enjoy. What the land was to Israel, Christ is to us. Mapped out in the pages of God's Word is all the territory which we are to possess: the mountains of heavenly vision; the valleys, at first seeming to be valleys of despair but which turn out to be valleys of infinite blessing;

the pasture lands of rest and quiet, the cities which must be conquered, the foes which must be overthrown. And it is true for every one of us that there is yet much land to be possessed. Our inheritance in Christ is not *part* of Christ, but *all* of Christ. All that there is in Jesus is God's purpose for us. Our possession is only that part of Christ which by faith we claim, and there is not one of us who can ever say that we have claimed all we should have.

Are we to be satisfied with less than God's will for us? We never reach a stage of Christian experience in which we exhaust all the possibilities of life in Jesus. Not one of us has won every battle that he has fought. As we go back over our experience, we cannot help but admit that our lives bear the scars of many a defeat. And we have not fought every battle that we should have fought, for there have been many times in our Christian living when we have evaded the enemy and chosen the easier path.

But I do not find these facts depressing. I find in them the inspiration that makes me cry, "Lord, lead me on to higher ground." For it is the experiences of defeat followed by the thrill of picking oneself up again and finding that the blood of Christ cleanses, and that the Saviour is at our hand and by our side and in our hearts to lead us on with Him—it is all this that keeps us pressing toward the goal. Christ never leaves us or forsakes us, but there is indeed much land yet to be possessed.

Let us think for a moment of some areas in your life and mine which are still to be possessed. Let us ponder how we may possess them, and, in conclusion, let us discover why it is that we do not possess them.

I suggest that there is much to possess in the realm of knowledge. I speak, of course, of knowledge as distinct from intellect. Mental discipline, memory, observation, all these things develop the intellect, but that is very different from knowledge. One may have little intellect, yet have a deep discernment of spiritual truth that goes beyond the limits of intellect. Some of the most wonderful confirmations and experiences of God's goodness have come while I was listening to a boy or girl who had had no educational advantages, but who had come to know in reality the presence and power of the indwelling Christ, and through Him to be able to speak with a wisdom beyond all intellect. On the other hand, of course, a man may be clever and very intellectual and very well informed, but have no knowledge at all; he may be a perfect fool in the things that matter most.

The Lord Jesus gives us eternal life that we may know the only true God. He bids us come to Calvary every day of our lives and with hushed spirits and awed hearts to gaze on Him who bled and died that we might be redeemed. If we see Him, we see the Father, for no man can understand the real heart of God except he gaze on a crucified, Risen Lord. Do we know Him? Can we say with the Apostle Paul, "I count all things but loss for the excellency of the knowledge of Christ Jesus my Lord: for whom I have suffered the loss of all things, and do count them but dung that I may win Christ. . . . That I may know him, and the power of his resurrection" (Phil. 3:8, 10)?

Oh, my dear friends, in the matter of the knowledge of Christ, how much land there is to be possessed! Why is it that we are so ignorant, really? Because we know so little of the Book. How many pages of your Bible are unpossessed, unexplored territory? How many of them have never been marked or underlined to show what God means to you? We go over the same portions again and again; we live in simple

ABC truths: in John 3 and other such chapters, great and wonderful, indeed, as they are. But whole continents of God's redemptive purpose, revealed for the enlightened mind to discover, to feed upon, and to rejoice in, are left unpossessed. You cannot know Jesus our Lord unless you know Him in His Word. Fellow Christians, venture into some unexplored field in the Word of God, and find what blessing there will be to follow.

There is also a wide area to be possessed in the realm of spiritual experience. In the life of every one of us, as indeed it was true in Canaan, are kings, enemies, strongholds, and habits which are deeply entrenched. They seem to be so strongly fortified that, in spite of every endeavor, in spite of all our prayers and Bible study, in spite of all our pleadings at the throne of God, it seems impossible to get rid of them. Our peace is constantly disturbed by the raids of an evil one inside our personality. He attacks us without warning, and in a moment we have lost our temper, have spoken sharply and critically. Time and time again, these enemies within have conquered in spite of years of Christian experience, or of lives on the mission field, or of leadership in Christian work, or of teaching other people. The enemy has captured us again and again, and his strongholds stand against all attempts we make to pull them down.

Is that true of you? If this book of Joshua, as we study it, means something to you, it means more and more to me every day, for I see in it the reflection of my own heart and my own life. If someone says to me, "This Christian life is a battle," my heart goes out to him, because I find it a battle, too. But, oh, thanks be to God for the victory in Jesus Christ when we learn how to claim it! How these areas of sin have resisted us! How these enemies have defied us! Somehow, like Israel, we fail to possess the land that God has given to us.

In some cases, of course, the reason is that the Christian has never handed over to the Lord Jesus his business life. He has kept it altogether outside the sphere of our Lord's authority and says, "I'll serve myself and my own ends. I'll make my money and look after my family and business, but that won't have anything to do with my religion." In other cases, it is because men are very reluctant to admit the authority of the Lord over worldly associations and worldly friends.

Oh, beloved, think of the ideal of God expressed to us in His Word, "That we might be conformed to the image of his Son"! Consider for a moment His strength and His sweetness, His holiness, His hatred of sin, His love for you and for me, His devotion to the will of God, His life of self-sacrifice. That is God's ideal, that is the ideal our souls must possess. If the life of our precious Lord is not being reproduced in us day by day, our Christianity is not vital, it is not effective, it is not revolutionary; for the sole purpose of our faith and the substance of all our doctrine is that we be conformed to the image of God's Son.

There is much land to be possessed! We know this is true. But how may we possess our possessions in Jesus Christ? Surely there is a means of achievement, and indeed there is! Let me show it to you and let me ask you carefully and prayerfully to consider it.

Remember that, first, we must be possessed by the Lord before we can know what it is in fullness to possess Him. "Not as though I had already attained," said the Apostle Paul (and I am so glad for the honesty of Paul's language—how can any man believe in sinless perfection when he reads the writings of Paul?). "either were already perfect: but I follow after, if that I may lay hold of that for which Christ Jesus laid hold of me" (Phil. 3:12) Yes, we first open our hearts to receive Him, and then, by a living faith, we appropriate Him.

Listen to the three great words of Christian experience in the order in which I give them to you: "surrender," "consecration," "appropriation." First, there must be utter submission to the Lord, and, let me repeat, there is no conversion without that absolute surrender of the will to the Lord Jesus Christ. Next, there must be the consecration of life and talents and everything that we have, in every department of life. Then comes appropriation by a living faith of the life that God sends by His Spirit through His Son. That is the divine order: we cannot possess the Lord Jesus in fullness until He possesses us. We cannot appropriate Christ until He has conquered our will and we are altogether His.

We need not look for victory in our lives until we come to Jesus in utter self-surrender. We expect the Lord Jesus Christ to lead us on to higher ground? We expect Him to give us victory? We expect to possess our possessions? It is only when in our hearts we have accepted the authority of God the Father, God the Son, and God the Holy Ghost, and every part of our being is yielded in unconditional surrender to the Trinity, that we may count on victory and seek to possess our possessions in Christ.

Why should we, like Joshua, become old and stricken in years and find much land to be possessed?

It may be only the author's flight of imagination, but, somehow, I picture that day when you and I individually will have a personal interview for the first time with the Lord in heaven. Oh, it will be so wonderful to see Him! When the struggles and the battles are ended, do you think that on that day He will show to us the pattern that He had for our lives from before the foundation of the world? Do you think He will show to us the place where we were side-tracked, the place where we lost, the place where by lack of faith and lack of obedience we went into some second best? Will He show us the place of His abundant mercy? Will we see more clearly than anywhere else in life that just there, where we slipped, He left the mark of His blood and the imprint of His hands on our lives as He held us when we sought to get out of His grip? All I pray is that on that day, for you as well as for me, if He does show us the blueprint of His plan for our lives, we shall discover by His grace that the actual experience was, in some measure at least, in line with that plan.

Why should we live in spiritual poverty? Why do we yield and fail? When this life is ended and this brief experience is over, when we are old, when the story is written and the battles are finished, why should we have to stand and face our Lord and confess that we have not possessed anything like what He intended us to have?

I believe that the answer to that question is in the sixth verse of this chapter, for the possession of the land was by lot. You will discover that the word "lot" occurs twenty-two times in the second half of the book of Joshua; possession of the land was by *lot*. God gave to each tribe that piece of territory, that difficult mountain, that heartbreaking experience, that sore trial that He knew in His wisdom would be eternally the best for it.

I believe that if we accept that truth we shall possess Christ in a new way. If we do not believe it and kick against our experience, if we refuse to accept God's portion, God's lot for our lives, then we will never possess the land. Abraham believed that: he let God choose for him in everything. His nephew Lot refused to believe it. The one walked by faith, the other by sight; one let God choose, the other made his choice himself. Mark the end of those men: the one who let God choose his lot entered into fullness of blessing; the other ended in disaster.

My Christian friends, are you letting God choose your lot in the inheritance, or do you make a plan of life for yourself? Do you choose your own path? Do you plan your career yourself? Do you trust to your own ingenuity or, in the words of a hymn that I love, have you ever said?—

Thy way, not mine, O Lord, however dark it be,
Lead me by Thine own hand; choose out the path for
me.

Smooth let it be or rough; it still will be the best;
Winding or straight it leads right onward to Thy rest.

I dare not choose my lot; I would not if I might;
Choose Thou for me, my God, so shall I walk aright.

Take Thou my cup, and it with joy or sorrow fill;
As best to Thee may seem, choose Thou my good and
ill.

Choose Thou for me my friends, my sickness or my
health;
Choose Thou my cares for me, my poverty or wealth.

Not mine, not mine the choice; in things or great or
small
Be Thou my guide, my strength, my wisdom, and my
all.

If you would possess your possessions, that is the answer!

# PART III

*Living the Life*

# CHAPTER 15

# THE SATISFIED LIFE

JOSHUA 13:33

*And Moses gave inheritance unto the half tribe of Manasseh: and this was the possession of the half tribe of the children of Manasseh by their families.*

*And their coast was from Mahanaim, all Bashan, all the kingdom of Og king of Bashan, and all the towns of Jair, which are in Bashan, threescore cities:*

*And half Gilead, and Ashtaroth, and Edrei, cities of the kingdom of Og in Bashan, were pertaining unto the children of Machir the son of Manasseh, even to the one half of the children of Machir by their families.*

*These are the countries which Moses did distribute for inheritance in the plains of Moab, on the other side Jordan, by Jericho, eastward.*

*But unto the tribe of Levi Moses gave not any inheritance: the Lord God of Israel was their inheritance, as he said unto them.*

JOSHUA 13:29–33

The first verse of chapter 13 of the book of Joshua begins with the Lord's reminder to Joshua: "There remaineth yet very much land to be possessed." We have seen how true that is in relation to the spiritual experience of us all. We remind ourselves that possession of the land by Israel was by lot. In other words, God determined the precise area which each tribe should occupy, and each was responsible for applying the principles the tribes had learned in united warfare to taking possession of the area which God had given it. We recognize that often it is because we refuse to accept our lot that we fail to possess all that God has for us in Christ.

I want to take up that thought and to say a word to those who are discontented with their lot. I come across many lonely lives today. Some are lonely because they are utterly disillusioned. Bright hopes of early years have been shattered. Ill health has dogged their footsteps, and they seem incapable of ever being, or doing, any good to anybody. In other cases, the marriage which began so hopefully has proved disastrous, and now they are left stunned amid the wreckage of what once was a home. Somehow, they feel they can never be the same again. Even some Christians look on them with suspicion, and the awful stigma of divorce seems to be beyond their power to remove.

Still others are facing life with no home at all. What was once a cherished dream has faded away, and they feel unwanted. Yet others have lost husband or wife, and are left with the care of children—utterly alone and crushed by the responsibility.

If during the years you have been tempted to build up what is almost a sense of resentment against God, and you are in danger of becoming bitter and sour, let me tell you that God has something to say to you from this portion of Scripture: "But unto the tribe of Levi Moses gave not any inheritance: the Lord God of Israel was their inheritance, as he said unto them" (Joshua 13:33).

If you link that verse with Deuteronomy 10:8 and 9, you will grasp something more of its significance. There you will read, "At that time the Lord separated the tribe of Levi, to bear the ark of the covenant of the Lord, to stand before the Lord to minister unto him, and to bless in his name, until this day. Wherefore Levi hath no part nor inheritance with his brethren; the Lord is his inheritance, according as the Lord thy God promised him." Great honor was allotted to these people, for they were called to a life of worship: the Lord God of Israel was their inheritance. They possessed Him—all His resources, all His power, all His blessings were to come to them, and then through them go to others. No relationship of secondary importance was to be allowed to hinder their communion with their God. He alone was their inheritance. Their interests were to be centered entirely in Him, and His service was to be undertaken without any distraction whatsoever.

The Levites were called, moreover, to a life of work. They were "to stand before the Lord to minister unto him." Their work was in the sanctuary, and their influence on others was that of the intercessor, the greatest influence in all the world. They were also called to a life of witness. They were "to bless in his name." They were to be, as it were, two-way channels, channels through which others could come to God, channels through which God could come to men.

At God's command, as we are told in Numbers 35:2, the other tribes were to set aside a total of forty-eight cities for the use of the Levites. When the Levites were free from the work of the sanctuary, they went to those cities to live. Fresh from the sanctuary of God, filled with the joy of His service and the glory of His presence, they brought the hallowing influence of the presence of the Lord everywhere they went. In the sanctuary they brought men to God; in the city they brought God to men. Such was the unique honor allotted to the Levites—a life of worship, a life of work, a life of witness. "The Lord God of Israel was their inheritance."

Is that the life to which some of you are being called? He has given you no inheritance in the land; yet He has given you all, for He is your inheritance. Can there be any frustration in that life? Does not that dissipate your resentment against God? Does not that open before you a new and limitless horizon, a life of boundless opportunity? Does not that remove the feeling of loneliness, and change the pain of being unwanted into a great thrill as you realize that Christ is yours and you are His? He wants you for Himself for the greatest service in all the world, to go into the sanctuary for men and to go out into the city for God.

In the second place, the history which prepared the tribe of Levi for this honor is of outstanding significance in the Old Testament. I want you to see what it was that led them to have this unique place in the economy of God. In Genesis 34:25-31 it is related that Simeon and Levi, brothers by birth, became involved in murder and were rebuked for it by their father, Jacob, who said that because of it they had dishonored his name among the people of the land. Even on his death bed, Jacob could never forget their cruelty, their anger, and their foul deeds, and, therefore, instead of pronouncing a father's blessing on them, he cursed them: "Instruments of cruelty are in their habitations. . . . Cursed be their anger, for it was fierce; and their wrath, for it was cruel: I will divide them in Jacob, and scatter them in Israel" (Gen. 49:5, 7).

There was nothing in the early years of Simeon and Levi which indicated God's future purpose. Their early life was shameful; they had brought disgrace on themselves, on their tribe, and on their families. But, my friends, is it not true that God restores the years that the cankerworm has eaten? Does He not take soiled hearts and cleanse them? Does He not take clay that has been marred in the hands of the potter and make it again another vessel? Yes, indeed He does! Never does our God allow past history, however unpleasant or however sinful, to prevent Him from allotting to us a unique place in His service.

Of course, there was a turning point. There came a moment when the curse on Levi was changed into a blessing. The curse on Simeon ran its course, and his tribe faded out of existence. But not so with Levi; the Lord God became the Levites' inheritance. How did that happen? In Exodus 32:26 we find the answer.

Moses, you remember, had returned from the mountain where he had received God's commandments, to find that all the people were given over to idolatry. He stood in the gate of the camp and cried to the whole army of his people, "Who is on the Lord's side? Let him come unto me." And to a man the Levites responded, repented of sin, and turned to God. From that moment they were marked out for blessing. It was then that God called them for priestly service, and decreed that He was to be their inheritance.

How different the fate of the two brothers! The one failed to repent, whereas the other repented, and inevitably the operation of God's government followed all through their lives. Please observe that the Levites made their choice of God, not when they were in the land of blessing, but when they were in the wilderness. Then God's promises seemed obscure and His purposes unknown. The future was dark and the journey wearisome. Sin and idolatry abounded all around them, and yet they turned to the Lord in that situation and sought His face. At that crucial, critical moment in their lives they chose the Lord.

What precious words God has to say to some of you from this story—indeed, to all of us! God chose you in Christ before the foundation of the world. He knew all about you before you were born; He watched you through your infancy and childhood, through your adolescence, through your early manhood or womanhood; never has there been a moment of your life when you were beyond His gaze or out of His care. Even when you turned from Him, His eye was always on you. Your journey may have been wearisome and lonely, difficult and dark, but, my friends, whatever the past held for you, remember, "He knoweth the way that I take."

Most especially does God recall when, in the wilderness, surrounded by sin and idolatry, you held out for Christ and refused to allow anything or anybody to pull you back into the world. Oh, how glad was the heart of God that day!

From then onward the question with which He has faced you is this: "Is it not lawful for me to do what I will with mine own?" Yes, in holding out for Christ you surrendered yourself to Him, and from that moment you were His.

To some, God has given no inheritance in the land, no home, no earthly love, only a way which seems full of hardship and crushing burdens. Perhaps you have come to believe that God has been punishing you for all your failure and reminding you that you are disqualified forever from His service because you bear a stigma upon you.

How different is the truth! The Lord God of Israel is your

inheritance. Yours is the unique privilege of testing the preciousness of the abounding grace of His pardon and His love. His offer to you is a life of worship, a life of work, and a life of witness if, out of the darkness of wilderness days, you chose Him as your undisputed Lord. To imagine, for instance, that a person who entered into a marriage that has proved disastrous must carry all through his life the stigma of it, is to place a burden on him which is utterly contrary to the Book and which the grace of Christ can utterly remove.

Thank God that in the moment when someone has been crushed seemingly beyond help, when the things that he has cherished most in life have crashed around him, and he is left in the shattered wreck of what once he thought was a home, the Lord Jesus holds out His hand to aid. Thank God, He takes the clay that has been marred, the precious, soiled, broken life, and molds it again, now into a vessel unto honor, sanctified, and meet for the Master's use. And He says, "From this moment onward the Lord thy God is thy inheritance."

I have sought to point out to you the honor which was allotted to the tribe of Levi and the history which prepared them for that honor. We must also observe the hope which that honor inspired in their hearts: "The Lord God of Israel was their inheritance, *as he said.*"

In other words, it was planned that it should be so. What happened to them was no mistake, no second best, but was in the counsel of a God whose ways are past finding out and whose wisdom is altogether perfect.

To put all the floodlight of truth on our text we need to remind our hearts again that the epistle of Paul to the church at Ephesus is the New Testament commentary on the book of Joshua. And in Ephesians 1:11–12 we read of the Lord Jesus

Christ, "in whom also we have obtained an inheritance, being predestinated according to the purpose of him who worketh all things after the counsel of his own will: that we should be to the praise of his glory, who first trusted in Christ." Do you get that language? "In whom we have obtained an inheritance"—a chosen inheritance, a lot, a portion ordained in the counsel of God, chosen according to His purpose, planned according to His purpose, planned according to His will, which is inscrutable. Why? In order "that we should be to the praise of his glory, who first trusted in Christ." That is our side of the picture, as it were. We have an inheritance in Jesus Christ; the Lord God of Israel is our inheritance.

But our side is to be matched by God's side; the partnership must be complete. The inheritance which we have in Jesus must have a response if there is to be perfection. That response is indicated in Ephesians 1:18, in which Paul prayed for his hearers, "The eyes of your understanding being enlightened; that ye may know what is the hope of his calling, and what the riches of the glory of his inheritance in the saints." Our inheritance in Christ is matched by Christ's inheritance in His people. Our possession of Him is to be matched by His possession of us.

It may be that you are not among the people about whom I have been thinking especially in this chapter. Of some of us it may be said, on the human level, that we have been more fortunate, because God has blessed us with happy homes and godly children, and enough of this world's goods to keep us from poverty. I speak to you as I would speak to my own heart: let us beware that the things which God has given us do not mar His inheritance in us and give Him a response in our hearts which is unworthy of His grace and His love.

To the lonely heart, to the disillusioned life, the life that has no inheritance in the land, God says, "The Lord thy God is thine inheritance." And that same God waits for you to answer Him and acknowledge that He has your heart wholly, that you are His without any question or dispute.

And of those of us whom God has blessed in human life with happy homes, it is still true that the Lord God of Israel is our inheritance. He is waiting until He finds an utter, complete inheritance in all His people. He has been denied that by some of us because of the very gifts He has given us. And I wonder if that is the reason why God often allows so many Christian hearts and homes that have been blessed with earthly things to go through darkness and terror to discover human, material things stripped from them. Maybe God has not been able to trust such people with these things, for they rob Him of His inheritance.

"The Lord God of Israel is thy inheritance!"

> Loved with everlasting love,
>   Led by grace that love to know,
> Spirit, breathing from above,
>   Thou hast taught me it is so.
> Oh, this full and perfect peace!
>   Oh, this transport all divine!
> In a love which cannot cease,
>   I am His, and He is mine.
>
> His forever, only His;
>   Who the Lord and me shall part?
> Ah, with what a rest of bliss
>   Christ can fill the loving heart.

Heaven and earth may fade and flee,
First-born light in gloom decline;
But, while God and I shall be,
I am His, and He is mine.

# CHAPTER 16

# THE DISCIPLE'S REWARD

### JOSHUA 14:14

*Then the children of Judah came unto Joshua in Gilgal: and Caleb the son of Jephunneh the Kenezite said unto him, Thou knowest the thing that the Lord said unto Moses the man of God concerning me and thee in Kadesh-barnea.*

*Forty years old was I when Moses the servant of the Lord sent me from Kadesh-barnea to espy out the land; and I brought him word again as it was in mine heart.*

*Nevertheless my brethren that went up with me made the heart of the people melt: but I wholly followed the Lord my God.*

*And Moses sware on that day, saying, Surely the land whereon thy feet have trodden shall be thine inheritance, and thy children's for ever, because thou hast wholly followed the Lord my God.*

*And now, behold, the Lord hath kept me alive, as he said, forty and five years, even since the Lord spake this word unto Moses, while the children of Israel wandered in the wilderness: and now, lo, I am this day fourscore and five years old.*

*As yet I am as strong this day as I was in the day that Moses sent me: as my strength was then, even so is my strength now, for war, both to go out, and to come in.*

*Now therefore give me this mountain, whereof the Lord spake in that day: for thou heardest in that day how the Ana-kims were there, and that the cities were great and fenced: if so be the Lord will be with me, then I shall be able to drive them out, as the Lord said.*

*And Joshua blessed him, and gave unto Caleb the son of Jephunneh Hebron for an inheritance.*

*Hebron therefore became the inheritance of Caleb the son of Jephunneh the Kenezite unto this day, because that he wholly followed the Lord God of Israel.*

*And the name of Hebron before was Kirjath-arba; which Arba was a great man among the Anakims. And the land had rest from war.*

JOSHUA 14:6–15

Chapter 14 of the book of Joshua contains a very wonderful story, the story of a man who, at the age of eighty-five, interrupted the apportionment of the land among the people of God when he stepped out of the ranks to claim the portion which God had promised to him forty-five years before.

Caleb is one of the great Bible characters. How deep, and yet how simple, was the secret of his greatness! Great people are not complicated; they are simplicity itself. You can read a real man of God like a book. To eyes that have been opened by the Spirit of God it is easy to discern such a man's greatness. How eternal are God's principles and how unchanging the conditions of all spiritual blessing! I am sure that if we learn wholly to follow the Lord our God as did Caleb, the result will be just the same in your life and mine. Caleb's God is our God.

That the faith which was ours in youth may be undimmed in old age, that the vision of the Lord shall be clearer as we grow older, that when life's journey is almost done we shall not be content merely to survey the past but be ready and eager still for fresh battles with the enemy—surely it is to all this that we aspire. It was the aspiration of this "Greatheart" of the Old Testament. Let us look at him, and see if we can understand the secret of his greatness.

This man of God had a faith that never wavered. Go back forty-five years to a fateful day in the history of God's people as recorded in chapters 13 and 14 of the book of Numbers. After a swift crossing of the wilderness they reached a place called Kadesh-barnea, on the very border of the land of God's promise. But the unbelief which had so often plagued them during the wilderness journey demanded that spies be sent in to survey the land. Twelve men, one from each tribe, you will remember, were sent to reconnoiter.

After a six-weeks' tour of inspection they brought back two reports: a majority report and a minority report. Now, the majority admitted that the land flowed with milk and honey, but spoke fearsomely of giants. "Nevertheless," they said, "the people be strong that dwell in the land, and the cities are walled, and very great; and we saw the children of Anak [which come of giants] there" (Num. 13:28). "We are not able to go up against" them, they said. The minority report brought by Caleb and Joshua admitted the existence of giants, but they believed God. "If the Lord delight in us, then he will bring us into this land" (Num. 14:8). "We are well able to overcome it," they said.

They had seen all that the majority had seen, with this difference: the majority measured the giants against their own strength; Caleb and Joshua measured the giants against

God. The majority trembled; the two triumphed. The majority had great giants but a little God. Caleb had a great God and little giants. Certainly there was an "if" in his belief, but it was not an "if" of unbelief but of humility: "If the Lord delight in us." As he said that, he looked back over a wilderness journey that had lasted a year; he recalled a day when he had been brought out of Egypt by the power of the blood of the Lamb; he remembered the sure leading of the pillar of fire by night and the cloud by day, and he knew that the Lord delighted in His people. "Therefore we are able to overcome."

The cry of the people was, "Let us go back to Egypt." They forgot its bondage. In their desire to avoid further trouble and peril in the journey they dishonored God. Therefore He made it perfectly plain that the land of blessing, which can be inherited only by faith and obedience, had to be refused to a whole generation of His people except Caleb and Joshua.

Of Caleb God had said, "Because he had another spirit with him, and hath followed me fully, him will I bring into the land whereinto he went" (Num. 14:24). How Caleb treasured that promise from the Lord in his heart during forty-five years of weary wandering, of incessant toil and ceaseless conflict, of unfulfilled hopes. Amid all the murmurings of the people he retained the fixed purpose wholly to follow the Lord. Like an illustrious ancestor, "he staggered not at the promise of God through unbelief; but was strong in faith, giving glory to God; . . . being fully persuaded that, what he had promised, he was able also to perform" (Rom. 4:20, 21). There was no use trying to involve Caleb in rebellion against Moses. Never was he found among the grumblers or among those who were skeptical and unbelieving. Never was he found among the people who hankered again for the leeks and garlic of Egypt. Never was he found among those who disobeyed God or among the people who turned to idolatry. He had caught a glimpse of the reward of obedience, and that was sufficient to keep him true for all the rest of his life, and until that brought him at last to the place that God had promised him.

What a moment when, at eighty-five years of age, that man, in all the maturity of godly character, and in all the authority of one who believed God, stepped out of the ranks alone! He had gone through many difficulties and succeeded in the struggle to overcome those who would have done almost anything to dissuade him from his conviction. What a thrill it was to hear him say, "Now, after forty-five years of waiting, after many an agony of soul, after having been tempted by the crowd to pull back—now, give me this mountain whereof the Lord spoke in that day!"

I do not know how many of us will live until we are eighty-five, but God knows how I long that when I come to the eventide of life I shall have a faith like Caleb's, a faith based on an unshakable conviction that the Lord delights in me. Doesn't He delight in us? Look back at Calvary's Cross. Surely God has shown His love toward us beyond all doubt, in that "while we were yet sinners, Christ died for us."

> I have caught a glimpse of Jesus,
> I care not for aught beside,
> So enchained my spirit's vision,
> Looking at the Crucified.

Because of that, no matter how dark or lonely the way, we know that God loves His people. We know that at the end of the journey the reward will be ours, that through faith and patience we shall inherit the promise. But, oh, how our faith wavers! How we shrink from the battle of life! We are not always on the alert; we are not always looking to Jesus. How, God forgive us, we have felt the lure of Egypt again! We have been conscious again and again of the fascination of things that we left in our youth. How often we have been discouraged in our struggle to go on with God. how often we have been tempted to complain, and how often, God forgive us, we have joined the host of those who grumble that the Christian life is too hard. We have to humble ourselves before God when we recognize that though we have been placed in position as His sons, in experience we are but sinners saved by grace.

My fellow Christians, I want you again to catch a glimpse of Jesus. Look back and remember the pit from which you were saved, look back at the peace that came into your life, and remind your heart that your faith is founded on the bedrock conviction that "God so loved the world that he gave his only begotten Son" (John 3:16).

Let us notice also that Caleb's strength never weakened. Verse 11 of this amazing chapter tells us that at the age of eighty-five Caleb declares that he is as strong as he was at forty. He said, "I am as strong this day as I was in the day Moses sent me: as my strength was then, even so is my strength now." A faith that never wavered had enabled him to lay hold on a strength that never weakened—the very power of God Himself. No human energy could suffice for all the trials of the way. Yet this man could toil and fight and exhaust himself, and still be full of the strength of God. If any man could say it, he could say that "though the outward man perisheth, yet the inward man is renewed day by day."

Oh, what a precious thing it is for me, in nearly middle

life, to meet those old enough to be my father or my mother, some of them shut-ins, frail in body, and unable to attend the house of God, some feeble in mind, but all strong in faith. I want to end my earthly journey like that, don't you? Strong, courageous, assured, bold in faith, and able to say, "I have fought a good fight, I have finished the course, and I have kept the faith." Caleb drew on a strength that was irresistible because he had a faith that never wavered.

And his reward was complete victory. In Joshua 15:14 we discover that of all the people who received an inheritance in the land, Caleb was the only one who succeeded in expelling the enemy. The others made poor headway; the last part of the book of Joshua makes sad reading, for over and over again we read, "They were not able to drive them out." The chariots of iron were too strong for them—often that is the record in the book. But Caleb drove out all the enemy, although there were three giants in the portion allotted to him. The man who wholly followed the Lord was the only one who was wholly victorious in the fight.

We are conscious—let us face this together in the presence of God—that so often have we failed to drive out the enemy. He is still lurking in a stronghold within us of which we are bitterly ashamed in our best moments. He still knows the weak points in our armor. But I have always found that failure to drive out the enemy in my life is always due to failure wholly to follow the Lord. There is some flaw, some draining away of spiritual strength, some sapping of spiritual vitality, or else the enemy would be exterminated. Absolute triumph is achieved only in response to utter obedience. God only knows, as He searches our hearts, the leakage in our consecration, the flaw in our obedience, the breakdown in following Him, which have resulted in our failure utterly to exterminate the foe. God forgive us, the Holy Spirit illumine our hearts! Caleb wholly followed the Lord, and he wholly drove out the enemy.

Now you must observe something else about Caleb, that he also had a blessing that never wasted. For again, in the 15th chapter, we are told that Caleb had something to spare for his daughter and her husband. He was able to portion out some of the inheritance that God had given to him, and to give it to this newly wedded couple as they set out together in life. He gave them the upper and the lower springs. Truly it might be said of Caleb that he was "like a watered garden, full of fragrance rare," such was the condition of his heart. The blessing of his life overflowed to other people, and he had the power to open springs of spiritual blessing for others.

Does your heart not hunger, and say, "Lord Jesus, make me like that"? Mine does. Oh to go into old age with radiance and the ability drawn from experience of the grace of God to pass on to some couple setting out on the journey through life the surplus that God has given to me! To be able to teach someone the way of grace and blessing and victory, and to be able to say these things unashamedly, not only with my lips, but with a life that has become sweet and gracious and Christlike—oh, for an old age like that!

Beloved, there was a secret to it, and it was simply this: Caleb had a love that never waned. When, at the age of forty, he toured and inspected the land, one place captured his heart. It was not its fruit, its milk and honey that appealed to him. To this giant of the faith such blessings were quite secondary. The name of the place was Hebron. Situated on a rugged mountain, it was the most powerful stronghold of the enemy, and was guarded by the strongest of the giants. There Abraham had pitched his tent. There God had spoken to

Abraham face to face. There God had given to Abraham the promise of the land. The word "Hebron" conveys within itself just this meaning: fellowship, love, and communion. That was the place that Caleb cherished. It is the place all of us must seek and find.

There is a place guarded by powerful forces, a rugged stronghold which Satan attempts to keep from God's people at all costs. He is prepared to barter portions of the land to the children of God: he will give them the plains and the valleys, he will give them milk and honey. Ah, but when Satan sees a soul pressing toward the mountain of Hebron—the soul that is going to be satisfied with nothing in his life other than love, fellowship, and communion with God—Satan is stirred to a last-ditch battle.

Here was the secret of Caleb's patience, of his faith, and of his complete victory—in Hebron he had caught a glimpse of the reward of discipleship—the greatest reward of all. Here God had met man face to face. Caleb saw the place of communion, of fellowship, of God's infinite blessing, and, regardless of the cost and the hardship, he pressed on until Hebron was his.

"Hebron therefore became the inheritance of Caleb the son of Jephunneh the Kenezite unto this day, because that he wholly followed the Lord God of Israel" (14:14).

# CHAPTER 17

# LIVING TO CAPACITY

JOSHUA 17:18

*And the children of Joseph spake unto Joshua, saying, Why hast thou given me but one lot and one portion to inherit, seeing I am a great people, forasmuch as the Lord hath blessed me hitherto?*

*And Joshua answered them, If thou be a great people, then get thee up to the wood country, and cut down for thyself there in the land of the Perizzites and of the giants, if mount Ephraim be too narrow for thee.*

*And the children of Joseph said, The hill is not enough for us: and all the Canaanites that dwell in the land of the valley have chariots of iron, both they who are of Beth-shean and her towns, and they who are of the valley of Jezreel.*

*And Joshua spake unto the house of Joseph, even to Ephraim and to Manasseh, saying, Thou art a great people, and hast great power: thou shalt not have one lot only:*

*But the mountain shall be thine; for it is a wood, and thou shalt cut it down: and the outgoings of it shall be thine: for thou shalt drive out the Canaanites, though they have iron chariots, and though they be strong.*

JOSHUA 17:14–18

The closing section of the book of Joshua, you will remember, deals with the principles of the possession of the land of Canaan by the children of Israel. It tells of the apportionment of the land among the tribes, and of the erection of the tabernacle in Shiloh, right in the very heart of the country, and names the cities of refuge appointed for the judgment of sin. There is a great deal that we could profitably learn from this apportionment of the land.

The tabernacle was placed in the center: God was in the midst of His people, around Him all gathered in worship—a reminder that it is the person of our blessed Lord Himself who is worshiped by the Christian. We do not worship a church or an ordinance: we worship God. We gather together Sunday by Sunday in the presence of our Lord, "For," He said, "where two or three are gathered together in my name, there am I in the midst of them" (Matt. 18:20).

Again, the tribes of the people of Israel were placed around the tabernacle; the portion each had in the land corresponded exactly to the position that had been allotted to it during the journey through the wilderness. Each tribe had its appointed place and portion, just as to each of us is given grace according to the measure of the gift of Christ. If only we would always bear in mind that grace is given according to the gift —not grace to match somebody else's gift, to do what somebody else is expected to do, but grace for the gift that God has given to each one of us.

However, I want to confine myself here to drawing your attention to some principles concerning the possession of our inheritance in Jesus Christ our Lord, as we learn a lesson from the experience of the children of Joseph as it is recorded in chapter 17 of Joshua.

First of all, then, we will look at the cause of their complaint. In verse 14: "The children of Joseph spoke unto Joshua saying, Why hast thou given me but one lot and one portion to inherit, seeing I am a great people, forasmuch as the Lord hath blessed me hitherto?" This tribe complained that they were a great people, and that they had not received a portion that was worthy of their greatness. They boasted that past blessings justified a greater reward. They suggested that they were really much too big for the little bit of land that had been given to them. They wanted more space, more elbow room, more room to grow and develop. Furthermore, they said, as we read in verse 16, that even in the small portion which had been allotted to them the Canaanites were strongly entrenched, and they had iron chariots, which presented an insurmountable obstacle. The enemy *would* dwell in the land.

Now, of course, the children of Joseph were among the people who had crossed over the Jordan; they had shared in the conquest of the land of Canaan. They were even Joshua's own tribe; it was from Ephraim, the son of Joseph, that Joshua came. Therefore they had important associations, of which they were very proud. So, because of their associations, they thought themselves to be a great people. But here the Holy Spirit of God throws the spotlight of heaven on them, separates them from the whole army of God's people, and assesses them at their own worth. They complained, "We haven't enough room!" The fact was that the enemy was deeply entrenched in the area which they did have.

The real value of Christian character can never be assessed in terms of membership in a church or a Christian community. The Holy Spirit deals with each one of us individually, at close quarters. You may travel through the world and claim to be a member of a famous church or organization, an association which may give you respect and even be held in awe by many people. But these things count for little or nothing in the sight of heaven. When the Spirit of God flashes His light into our souls we lose the halo which our associations give us, and we find that God is dealing with us singly. Greatness has nothing to do with church associations. It has everything to do with faithfulness to the Lord and constant, persistent endeavor after holiness of life.

How often is this situation with which the children of Joseph were faced repeated in lives today! The children of Joseph were not satisfied with their lot; there was not enough scope for their gifts they thought; they wanted a larger sphere of service. Yet the fact of the matter was that in the sphere which God had given them the enemy was still deeply entrenched.

Your complaint may be the same—that you do not have enough scope for your own abilities. Are you constantly discontented with your present lot? Do you often pine for a greater opportunity to serve the Lord? Is your heart set on some mission field? For it may be that the searchlight of God's Word will disclose that the enemy is still deeply entrenched in your soul. May the Spirit of God point out to you that perhaps you have not really possessed the lot which God has given you.

"The Canaanites would dwell in the land," the enemy has been desperately persistent, and the truth of the matter is that you cannot drive them out. How often you say, "If only I could get away from my home! If only circumstances were different! If only I could move from this little job; it is not nearly big enough for me. I am worth so much more than this restricting, frustrating opportunity that God has given to me."

As God speaks to you today, do you not see that the real trouble in your life may be, not that you have not enough scope for your gifts, but that you are not living to capacity where you are? Satan is still sharing the land with you. You may want to leave him behind and move on to greater things, but that is never God's way. You can strain at the leash just as long as you like, but God's Spirit will hold you back and focus the searchlight of the Word on your life. He will keep you where you are until you have occupied and lived to capacity just there, and until—in the place in which you are serving, in the lot that He has given you, up to the capacity of your heart for Christ—the enemy has been vanquished.

Of course, you could ignore all this, and fling off God's restraint; you could take the bit between your teeth, as it were, and refuse God's discipline. You could plunge into some greater sphere; you could make your application to your missionary society, and go out to some foreign country; but, unless you live to capacity in your present sphere, you will be doomed to tragedy when you get there. The end would be tragedy, not only for yourself, but for other people if, unknown to your mission board, unknown indeed to anybody but God and yourself, the enemy in your heart had never been vanquished, the flag of victory never unfurled in your life.

There is a challenge here to capacity living, arising out of the complaint of these people in this portion of God's Word.

"Well," somebody says to me, "I see that, and I realize it, but how is it all going to be accomplished?" Let me ask you to look now at the call to personal conquest. Please observe, in verse 15, how Joshua dealt with his complaint: "If you are a great people"—I can't help thinking there was a touch of sarcasm there—"If you say you are so great, if you think you are so wonderful, then there is plenty of unoccupied land within the limits of your present lot. Even though it be forest land," said Joshua, "cut down the trees."

"Yes," replied the children of Joseph, "that is all very well, but the truth of the matter is that even with the trees cut down we would still need more room. The hill country is not enough—the enemy is entrenched in the valley, and he has iron chariots."

"Very well," said Joshua, "you are a great people, are you not? If you have such great power, use it! The mountains shall be yours—cut down the trees. The valley shall be yours"—in the words of Joshua 17:18—"for thou shalt drive out the Canaanites, though they have iron chariots, and though they be strong."

Do you see the shattering revelation? We may claim to have great associations; we may claim the halo of these associations and say we are a great people. "All right," says the Lord. "You think you are great; drive out the foe. What are you doing about it where you are, in the lot which has been given to you?" The call of the Word is the constant, relentless, personal, ceaseless call to conflict and to conquest. "Cut down the wood," says the Word of God. Faith must strike at the very root of sin; the dead wood must go. The seeming impossibilities which face us are only to show what God can do in answer to our faith, for within us is all the power of His indwelling Spirit.

The Lord says to some one of you who may be looking for new spheres and new opportunities and greater doors of service, "What about the trees in your life which mar your vision, which block your progress, which rob you of your victory? Cut them down!" Have you allowed the Cross of Christ to go right down to the root of sin and corruption? Have you asked the Lord to lay the ax to the very root of it in your life?

We all know these things which rob us of our blessing and of our victory. Says the Lord, "If you are a great and powerful people, then use the power and strike with the ax of the Word at the very root of sin in your life." For there is no wider sphere of service and there is no greater opportunity to be entrusted to us until we learn that lesson. Stop crying for greater opportunities until you have done the work in the place that God has allotted to you. Is your home sweeter and lovelier and more radiant because you are a Christian? If it is not, then lay the ax to the root of the tree and cut out the thing that hinders. Drive out the enemy! For if we fail in the small portion allotted to us God can never trust us with greater.

In the light of the Cross, is it not true that the enemy has no right to dwell in the land? Is it not true that his claim to your life was taken from him at Calvary? Is it not true that sin has no right to a foothold in the life of the child of God? Is it not true that Satan has no power in the presence of Omnipotence? Is it not true that by virtue of His blood and His resurrection, Jesus Christ is pledged to destroy the enemy utterly? Is it not true that in the indwelling power of the Holy Spirit there is strength for every temptation, grace for every trial, power to overcome every difficulty?

Truly, thank God, we are a great people, not in the sense that the children of Joseph used that word, because they thought that their greatness was due to their own importance, reputation, and associations, but because in our hearts and lives are the power, the authority, and the sovereignty of our precious Lord. When by His power you have possessed your present sphere and have overcome the enemy where you are, then He will enlarge your opportunity. With the greater opportunity for service will come the greater inflow of the power of God. Maybe the limited opportunity with which God entrusts us is restricted because we have called on only limited supplies of grace, for there is grace to match every task in the will of God.

Let the Christian begin to plead that the Lord will enlarge his capacity for Jesus, and make the prayer of his life, "O God, make me more like my Saviour." Let the Christian cry to God that the Holy Spirit increase his capacity, and he will soon discover that the increased grace will then merit increased opportunity. Do you see that principle? Let me remind you that your capacity for the indwelling Christ is not incapable of expansion. The capacity for Christ's indwelling is elastic: it increases as the years go by.

Recently I was reading some of the memoirs of Robert Murray McCheyne, that great man of God who passed on to glory when he was only thirty years of age and left behind him such a tremendous record of ministry and service. In his own prayer life McCheyne prayed, "Lord Jesus Christ, let my heart and my mind enlarge together like brother and sister, depending the one upon the other. Let the capacity of my heart and the understanding of my mind increase as the years go by." That is blessedly true of Christian experience. Some people claim that they are filled with the Spirit of God. My friends, that is a blessed truth, and I hope that all of us can say it sincerely, but we are filled only to the amount of our capacity. There is always more of His fullness as the years unfold, and you will never plumb all the depths of the ocean of His grace and power.

Yes, your capacity for grace can increase, and when grace increases, your heart expands, and then God can entrust you with a greater sphere of opportunity. Some people complain of their lot and say they are too big for the little job that God has given them to do. They want bigger things. My friends, God will hold you where you are until you have learned to receive greater power and grace. And the more grace, the more expansion of heart, the more love, the more fruit of the Holy Spirit revealed in your life, the greater and more wonderful and more effectual will be the doors of service He will open for you.

If somebody asks me, "How does my heart expand to receive more and more of Jesus?" my answer is this: The capacity to receive the grace of God and the indwelling of His Holy Spirit is measured by the character of your obedience and your faith. If you want more of Him, then cut down the dead wood. Get rid of the thing that robs you of your victory, and grace will be poured into your life.

For the greater the obedience, the greater the discipline, the greater the faith, the fuller and more complete the allegiance to our precious Lord, the more does the heart expand to receive more and more of Jesus. That capacity life has no limit; you will grow in it, until sometimes you will feel ready to burst—but that will not happen! For as you go on and on with the Lord Jesus Christ and obey Him today up to the hilt, then tomorrow there will be enlargement of heart and a further call to fresh obedience. That is Christian living.

Obey God in all things today! Drive out the enemy! Lay the ax to the root of the tree, and the capacity for Jesus Christ will be increased tomorrow. Always the soul of the Christian either grows or shrinks; it never remains the same. Either it increases in capacity for life because it obeys and is determined to lay the ax to the root of sin, or it shrivels until the Christian experience is lost behind a cold steel wall of doctrine and dogma.

There is a very wonderful paradox which you will always find to be true. Note it as you witness the lives of other people and, best of all, as you examine your own. He in whose life grace increases will, at the same time, become smaller in himself. You do not notice him so much; you see the Lord. But he who rejects the path of obedience and discipline, who does not put the ax to the root of sin in his own life, who refuses to go all the way in allegiance to the Lord, becomes smaller spiritually; his capacity for life shrivels up, and the grace of God within him is less and less revealed. His only increase is in self-esteem.

Watch a Christian grow! Watch yourself grow! If we do not face, in our own lives, the real implications of this message, we will shrivel up spiritually. Christian growth depends on whether we expand spiritually, and so receive more grace, and therefore may be entrusted by Father, Son, and Holy Spirit with a greater sphere of service, opportunity, and testimony.

# CHAPTER 18

## PERILS TO AVOID

### JOSHUA 18:3

*And the whole congregation of the children of Israel assem
bled together at Shiloh, and set up the tabernacle of the congregation there. And the land was subdued before them.*

*And there remained among the children of Israel seven
tribes, which had not yet received their inheritance.*

*And Joshua said unto the children of Israel, How long are
ye slack to go to possess the land, which the Lord God of
your fathers hath given you?*

JOSHUA 18: 1–3

*The Lord also spake unto Joshua, saying,*

*Speak to the children of Israel, saying Appoint out for you
cities of refuge, whereof I spake unto you by the hand of
Moses:*

*That the slayer that killeth any person unawares and un-
wittingly may flee thither: and they shall be your refuge
from the avenger of blood.*

*And when he that doth flee unto one of those cities shall
stand at the entering of the gate of the city, and shall declare
his cause in the ears of the elders of the people, they shall*

*take him into the city unto them, and give him a place, that he may dwell among them.*

*And if the avenger of blood pursue after him, then they shall not deliver the slayer up into his hand; because he smote his neighbour unwittingly, and hated him not beforetime.*

*And he shall dwell in that city, until he stand before the congregation for judgment, and until the death of the high priest that shall be in those days: then shall the slayer return, and come unto his own city, and unto his own house, unto the city from whence he fled.*

JOSHUA 20: 1–6

*And the children of Reuben and the children of Gad and the half tribe of Manasseh returned, and departed from the children of Israel out of Shiloh, which is in the land of Canaan, to go unto the country of Gilead, to the land of their possession, whereof they were possessed, according to the word of the Lord by the hand of Moses.*

*And when they came unto the borders of Jordan, that are in the land of Canaan, the children of Reuben and the children of Gad and the half tribe of Manasseh built there an altar by Jordan, a great altar to see to.*

. . . . .

*And they came unto the children of Reuben, and to the children of Gad, and to the half tribe of Manasseh, unto the land of Gilead, and they spake with them, saying,*

*Thus saith the whole congregation of the Lord, What trespass is this that ye have committed against the God of Israel, to turn away this day from following the Lord, in that ye have builded you an altar, that ye might rebel this day against the Lord?*

. . . . .

*Then the children of Reuben and the children of Gad and the half tribe of Manasseh answered, and said unto the heads of the thousands of Israel,*

*The Lord God of gods, the Lord God of gods, he knoweth and Israel he shall know; if it be in rebellion, or if in transgression against the Lord, (save us not this day,)*

*That we have built us an altar to turn from following the Lord, or if to offer thereon burnt offering or meat offering, or if to offer peace offerings thereon, let the Lord himself require it;*

*And if we have not rather done it for fear of this thing, saying, In time to come your children might speak unto our children, saying, What have ye to do with the Lord God of Israel?*

*For the Lord hath made Jordan a border between us and you, ye children of Reuben and children of Gad; ye have no part in the Lord: so shall your children make our children cease from fearing the Lord.*

*Therefore we said, Let us now prepare to build us an altar, not for burnt offering, nor for sacrifice:*

*But that it may be a witness between us, and you, and our generations after us, that we might do the service of the Lord before him with our burnt offerings, and with our sacrifices, and with our peace offerings; that your children may not say to our children in time to come, Ye have no part in the Lord.*

. . . . .

*And Phinehas the son of Eleazar the priest, and the princes, returned from the children of Reuben, and from the children of Gad, out of the land of Gilead, unto the land of Canaan, to the children of Israel, and brought them word again.*

*And the thing pleased the children of Israel; and the children of Israel blessed God, and did not intend to go up against them in battle, to destroy the land wherein the children of Reuben and Gad dwelt.*

*And the children of Reuben and the children of Gad called the altar Ed: for it shall be a witness between us that the Lord is God.*

JOSHUA 22:9, 10; 15, 16; 21–27; 32–34

Seven years of fighting for the possession of Canaan by the people of God is now over at this stage of the book of Joshua. Jordan has been crossed and Jericho has been conquered; the enemy has been routed, and the land has been allotted to the people according to their tribes. But now the most important part of the whole business confronts them, for their crossing over the river into the land of blessing and their victory over the enemy will prove utterly abortive unless they learn how to live in the land.

What was true of the children of Israel is a thousand times truer of Christian people today. The Christian life is not intended to be a series of crises and emotional upheavals. The Christian life in the purpose of God is expected to be a steady, onward, triumphant march toward the goal, the very presence of God. Of course, there are essential crises in the process. Jordan must be crossed; the wilderness of defeat must be exchanged for the country of blessing and victory. The enemy must be subdued; the Christian must learn how daily to conquer the enemy of his soul.

But, most important of all, the child of God, if he is entering into the land of full salvation, has to learn how to stay there. Though a man who has been born again of the Spirit of God and redeemed by the blood of Christ, will, I believe, be eternally saved, he may, nevertheless, move out from Canaan into the wilderness. He may move out of victory into defeat. He may run well for a while and cross Jordan, and claim himself to be buried with Christ and risen with Him too, but end the journey of his life on the very verge of Egypt itself. It is absolutely vital that the Christian should learn how to live in the land of blessing.

One lesson on that was learned, I trust, in the last chapter, when we thought together about living to capacity. We discovered that daily obedience to, and faith in, Christ serves to enlarge our capacity for His indwelling life, so that we may be filled with the Spirit of God one day and yet have more of that fullness the next.

The remainder of the book of Joshua has to do with three particular secrets of how to live in the land of blessing. Chapters 18 to 22 tell us of perils to avoid. Chapter 23 speaks to us of principles to follow. Chapter 24, the last chapter of the book of Joshua, reveals to us some privileges we may enjoy.

I do trust that we have learned some great principles of Christian living in these chapters: the way to victory, the way to enter into the land of full salvation. The Christian should never rely on past decisions or on mountain-top experience. He has to translate all that into the humdrum of daily living. That is one of the biggest lessons a missionary has to learn. Some who leave the homeland with all the thrill of valedictory services, and think that all they have to do is to stand up and lead hundreds of natives to Christ, are going to suffer shattering disillusionment when they reach the foreign field. They will find that a good deal of their time must be spent doing the daily chores, and unless they are prepared for such service they will go down.

How to live in the land of blessing is an essential theme for all of us, wherever God may have us live in the land. To meet a Christian who is really living the Christian life is one of the most thrilling experiences imaginable. It is so thrilling because, alas, it is so rare. To meet a Christian who is really enjoying his salvation and living in spiritual power to the full is a benediction. If we would live in the land and enjoy it all, and understand the possibilities of Christian living this side of glory, I want to show you three perils that all of us must avoid.

Joshua 18:3 leads us to the first of them: "And Joshua said unto the children of Israel, How long are ye slack to go in to possess the land which the Lord God of your fathers hath given you?" The first peril of the child of God is the peril of inertia.

You remember that before the children of Israel entered into the land Moses gathered them all together and spoke to them concerning the blessing that awaited them if they obeyed the Lord and went right into the land and possessed it. For instance, of Benjamin he said, "The beloved of the Lord shall dwell in safety by him . . . between his shoulders" (Deut. 33:12). What a place to live! In safety by the Lord—between the shoulders of the Master!

Of the tribe of Issachar Moses said they would receive the deep treasures of the ocean, and discover the jewels of the sands. For the tribe of Issachar were some very, very precious gifts if they possessed the portion that was allotted to them. The child of God who would possess all that is his in Christ will have limitless experiences of the fathomless ocean of the grace of God, and some of the most wonderful jewels of Christian character will be his.

The tribe of Asher, Moses said, would live in a particular part of the land which would be full of winepresses. Their feet would move in oil. "Thy shoes shall be iron and brass," so strong were they, and, said Moses to them, "as thy days, so shall thy strength be" (Deut. 33:24, 25). The tribe of Asher would never become old and weary and downhearted. They would be perennially fresh and strong. For His children God has oil, the unction of His Spirit; He constantly renews strength and power for every situation all through the journey of life.

The tribe of Naphtali, Moses said, would be full of the blessing of the Lord and be utterly satisfied. And so we could go on. Enough to show you that this people had the prospect of immense experiences: safety, unction, power, blessing, limitless grace, and strength. All these would be theirs if only they would go in and possess them, and, asks Joshua, as he witnesses this great company of people that had crossed Jordan and subdued the enemy beginning to settle down, "How long will ye be slack to go in to possess what the Lord God of your fathers has given you?"

My dear Christian friends, there is an experience of Christ for us, a share in His victory, an experience of the fullness of His blessing that is as far beyond the level of average Christian living as Canaan was beyond the wilderness.

There is a special little bit of land in this world which has for me very precious memories. It covers an area of about eighty miles south of the English-Scottish border. There you can walk over the ruins of Hadrian's wall, once the limits of the Roman empire in England. You can conjure up in your mind the tremendous events of those days when the power of Rome reached that very spot.

If you go round that district you will find very many old and ancient towers, some of them in complete ruins, others of them beautifully preserved almost as they were. If you ask

why it is that some of them are in ruins and some are in good
condition, you would be told this story. Several hundred
years ago England and Scotland were at bitter enmity, and
the English in Northumberland were constantly being attacked by the Scots, who carried away their cattle and stole
their crops. Therefore the English built castles near the
border to defend themselves. Some of those castles had secret
springs that provided a constant flow of water. Other castles
had to receive their water supply through a pipe from a well
many hundreds of yards away. The Scottish invaders were
astute enough to know what to do—they would cut the pipe,
then sit around the fortress and wait until the people inside
died of starvation and thirst. But those who had a secret
spring in their castles were invincible. So those castles stand
until this day as living reminders of their invincibility. The
other castles lie in ruins.

Every one of us has within him a fountain of life, but
there are Christians who have not discovered it. Many are
always going outside themselves: outside for amusement and
ease, for luxury and indulgence, and, before long, their
Christian life stands in utter ruins. But there are other children of God who have learned that the only way of possessing the land and holding on to the grace which God in Christ
has given them is to draw continuously on the inner secret
fountain of life. They can say with all their hearts that Jesus
satisfies.

The trouble is that so many of us shrink from pressing into
that land of blessing because we know it means self-denial
and the sacrifice of some pet habit or sin. It means that our
love of ease, our attachment to the world, and our dread of
being thought peculiar by other people, will all have to be
cast aside. It is these things that keep us spiritually slack and

inert, so that we don't move in to possess what God has for us.

How easily does the child of God rest satisfied with past achievements! What a tragedy that is, for not only does he rob himself of the blessing of God, but he hinders other people and encourages Satan. No Christian will win the race if he stops to take a breather. No one will win the war if, on the very verge of victory, he asks for a furlough. No child of God can afford to take one minute's vacation from walking with God. How sad that so many of us have the prize almost within our grasp, the goal almost within reach, only to discover that we have come short of it and of the victory that could have been ours in Jesus Christ! We lost simply because we did not press home to possess what God had for us. We were overcome by inertia.

Christians, how long is it since you went to church on Sunday mornings and *expected* God to bless you? You went just to do your job, to sing, to lead your Sunday-school class, to give out your notices, to take your part, to do your ushering—God bless you for it all—but beware of succumbing to spiritual inertia. Do not cease expecting God, who did great things in past generations, to do them again. He is able; if only we could get the hearts of people hungry and eager to press right home for what He has. So often the danger is laziness: "I don't care"; "I don't bother these days"; or "Well, it is all very well for other people, for the younger people, for children, but not for me." How long, my fellow Christians, how long will you be slack to possess what God has for you in Jesus? Oh, what a peril to avoid!

The second peril is recorded in Joshua 22; I call it the peril of incompatibility. You know what that means—inability to get on with other people.

Here is the story, briefly told in a sentence or two: The two and a half tribes, Reuben, Gad, and half the tribe of Manasseh, had seven years previously staked a claim to live on the other side of the river, on the wilderness side of Jordan. Joshua agreed that they should do so on one condition: that they should come into the land with the rest, and help subdue the enemy, after which they could return to the portion they wanted. In this chapter is the account of how they did that. Joshua publicly acclaimed their goodness, their generosity, and their spirit of fellowship in helping their brethren conquer the land, and wished them God's richest blessing in their appointed territory.

When the departing tribes came to the border, to the brink of the river, as recorded in chapter 22:24, they suddenly bethought themselves, "Now, suppose we go back to the other side of this river, our children and future generations will say, concerning us, 'What have you got to do with the people of God, anyway? They live over there, you live here. You have nothing to do with them, for you never did any of the fighting, you never helped subdue the enemy. Why, what have you got to do with the people of Israel?' " And so they erected an altar on the very westward brink of Jordan, not for sacrifice, but as a witness to their oneness with the people on the other side of Jordan.

When the other tribes heard what was happening, they immediately jumped to false conclusions and presumed that this altar was for worship and sacrifice, that it showed division among the people of God, that it indicated that these two and a half tribes who were departing from them were apostate, and no longer worshiping God, but rebellious against Him and indifferent to His law. Therefore they presumed there was schism right in the very heart of the people of God. So the tribes which had remained with Joshua in Canaan prepared to attack the supposed apostates.

Before doing so, however, they sent up a committee to discover exactly what the Reubenites, the Gadites, and the half tribe of Manasseh were doing, and to complain very frankly of their action. The committee accused them of being disloyal and in rebellion against God, and warned them of the awful consequences to them and to all Israel if they continued in their action. Those two and a half tribes had, in fact, no trouble at all in convincing the committee that their motives were perfectly pure, and that they had not intended their altar for worship, but as a testimony. They were not going to sacrifice to another God; they were simply raising a witness which declared their unity with their brethren. This easily proved that their motive was pure and sincere, and that the others were completely wrong in their judgment. What might have ended in tragedy ended, indeed, in closer ties of fellowship!

What lessons we have just here! What peril lies in the incompatibility of Christian with Christian! How easily misunderstandings occur, and with what damaging results! How rapidly they spread, and the farther they go the worse they get, until often an evangelical church is completely ruined by this very sin. Why is it we are all so ready to listen to gossip? Why is it that we are so quick to impute the worst motives to other people? Why do we believe so quickly a rumor concerning another person's character, and then repeat it with hundredfold exaggeration?

If only this sort of business were cleared out of the church, if only the Church of Christ today were utterly delivered from this deadly sin, we would have revival. It is the gossiper, he who imputes false motives, who puts the ugliest interpre-

tation on innocent actions, whom the devil is using as his tool
in Christian churches today. It is not much good—indeed, it
is no use at all—to go into raptures about the sermon on Sunday morning if you are not prepared to remove the causes of
your estrangement from your brother Christian.

Perhaps some who read this are sick at heart and broken in
spirit because of the false judgment and unjust treatment
that some fellow believer has given them. They are not singing hymns; they are suffering cruelly, and the wound that
has been inflicted has hurt and gone deep. However, though
they are suffering, they are growing; while the people who
come and sing hymns Sunday after Sunday and have the
spirit of resentment within them are backsliding spiritually.
Oh, the people we have misunderstood and wounded, the
people we have hurt and grieved, the people we have mis-
judged! And they have learned by the grace of God to take
it, and because of that are growing in grace. And we, if we
have been resentful and unkind, are shriveling spiritually.
On the mission field, or in the same town, or even perhaps in
the church building worshiping with you, are men and
women wounded bitterly, but, by the grace of God, growing in Jesus Christ.

Let me say to you (and perhaps this comes from personal
experience more than from anything else) that many of us
begin life by being harsh in our judgments, and white-hot in
our anger, and impetuous in our decisions; but, by the grace
of God, though we cannot yield one inch of allegiance to
the truth, we can learn to deal gently with the brother who
has fallen. We can learn to help him to carry the load and
bear the burden; in a spirit of meekness we can restore him
and count it the greatest of all gains, not to overcome him in

argument, or to destroy him by sarcasm, but to win him in love back to Jesus. Oh, the peril of incompatibility!

The third peril I discover in the 20th chapter, and it is a deadly danger to life in the land of blessing. It is the peril of ignorance.

You remember the establishment of the cities of refuge reported in this chapter: there were six of them, three on each side of the river. All were easy of access to everybody in the land and to the two and a half tribes on the other side of the river. They were places of refuge for anybody who had unintentionally killed someone. You will find full details in Deuteronomy 19. Enough here to say that sins of ignorance or of accident, sins that were unintentional, with no malice, were dealt with mercifully. The unfortunate man had only to flee to a city of refuge to be free from vengeance. There he would have his case judged by the Levites, and if it was proved that he was innocent of any malice in his action, he was permitted to stay in the city of refuge until the high priest of his time had died. Then he was free to return home in safety.

Do you ever stop to think that much of our guilt is due to ignorance? Do we understand that anything contrary to God's perfect holiness is sin? Do we understand that we are constantly grieving Him with our carelessness, our haste, and our misunderstanding of others? It may not be intentional; nevertheless, in God's sight it is sin. Oh, how we should thank Him for forgiveness!

We can go today to a fountain and there cleanse ourselves of sin and receive forgiveness for the unintentional hurt and harm that we have caused to others. For our city of refuge is the wounded side of Jesus, our High Priest, who died and rose again. A visit to the city of refuge, confession of our guilt, and cleansing by the blood will enable us to go free in perfect faith. How much we need today to go to Him with our best and blundering attempts to serve God, for our service is always unprofitable. How desperately we need to go to Him to rid ourselves of ignorance of His Word, His will, and His grace! In our city of refuge we shall always be safe, for our High Priest lives forever.

## CHAPTER 19

# PRINCIPLES TO FOLLOW

JOSHUA 23:11

*And it came to pass a long time after that the Lord had given rest unto Israel from all their enemies round about, that Joshua waxed old and stricken in age.*

*And Joshua called for all Israel, and for their elders, and for their heads, and for their judges, and for their officers, and said unto them, I am old and stricken in age:*

*And ye have seen all that the Lord your God hath done unto all these nations because of you; for the Lord your God is he that hath fought for you.*

*Behold, I have divided unto you by lot these nations that remain, to be an inheritance for your tribes, from Jordan, with all the nations that I have cut off, even unto the great sea westward.*

*And the Lord your God, he shall expel them from before you, and drive them from out of your sight; and ye shall possess their land, as the Lord your God hath promised unto you.*

*Be ye therefore very courageous to keep and to do all that is written in the book of the law of Moses, that ye turn not aside therefrom to the right hand or to the left;*

*That ye come not among these nations, these that remain among you; neither make mention of the name of their gods, nor cause to swear by them, neither serve them, nor bow yourselves unto them:*

*But cleave unto the Lord your God, as ye have done unto this day.*

*For the Lord hath driven out from before you great nations and strong: but as for you, no man hath been able to stand before you unto this day.*

*One man of you shall chase a thousand: for the Lord your God, he it is that fighteth for you, as he hath promised you.*

*Take good heed therefore unto yourselves, that ye love the Lord your God.*

*Else if ye do in any wise go back, and cleave unto the remnant of these nations, even these that remain among you, and shall make marriages with them, and go unto them, and they to you:*

*Know for a certainty that the Lord your God will no more drive out any of these nations from before you; but they shall be snares and traps unto you, and scourge in your sides, and thorns in your eyes, until ye perish from off this good land which the Lord your God hath given you.*

*And, behold, this day I am going the way of all the earth: and ye know in all your hearts and in all your souls, that not one thing hath failed of all the good things which the Lord your God spake concerning you; all are come to pass unto you, and not one thing hath failed thereof.*

*Therefore it shall come to pass, that as all good things are come upon you, which the Lord your God promised you; so shall the Lord bring upon you all evil things, until he have destroyed you from off this good land which the Lord your God hath given you.*

*When ye have transgressed the covenant of the Lord your God, which he commanded you, and have gone and served other gods, and bowed yourselves to them; then shall the anger of the Lord be kindled against you, and ye shall perish quickly from off the good land which he hath given unto you.*

JOSHUA 23:1–16

Chapter 23 of the book of Joshua brings us to a time when more than twenty years have passed since the Israelites entered the land of Canaan. The intensity of that campaign, the responsibilities of leadership, and the passing of years had all taken their toll of their great warrior leader and left their mark on him. Now we find that he himself has said he was old and stricken in age. All around him he had seen people he had led into the land of blessing settling down, apparently content to share the occupation of the land with the people whom God had commanded them to drive out.

As the time of his earthly life was drawing to a close, Joshua sensed the danger of their compromise and he confronted the people. He called their leaders first, and then the rank and file, to give each a farewell message. You can picture the scene as the great old warrior addressed his people. Caleb would be among them. Phinehas the high priest would be there. Many who had shared every battle since the day they crossed the Jordan, and had stood with their leader through thick and thin, would be present. Others would be there also: the younger generation aspiring to leadership, eager to press on in life and conquest.

In his address to the leaders Joshua told them of the principles they must follow if they were to establish their hold on the land of blessing. Then he spoke (chapter 24) to the rank and file concerning promises that they might claim if they wished all their hopes to materialize. My heart thrills as I listen to him speaking of the faithfulness of God through all the years that have gone and saying, "Not one thing hath failed of all the good things which the Lord your God spake concerning you" (23:14).

I wish that I might speak to you out of such ripe and mature experience as Joshua's. How I would wish that one could even come back from eternity to speak for a few moments concerning the things of God! There are some things that a middle-aged man can say in the midst of the conflict and the battle of the years that afford inspiration and help. But best of all is to listen to the ripe experience of a man who has been through the conflict of everyday life, and is soon to retire from the scene. I would give anything to sit at the feet of such a man.

But that is all wishful thinking and utterly impossible. I must ask you, therefore, to bear with me while I seek to set before you some principles to follow if you would live daily in the land of God's salvation. I would speak primarily to those of you in Christian leadership and to those of you who are training for it—to ministers, missionaries, church officers and leaders. Perhaps we might learn together from this great warrior Joshua, as the Holy Spirit teaches us, some more of the great principles for living in the land of blessing.

First of all, Joshua addressed the people on the danger of apostasy. His great concern seemed to be that seven nations still shared the land of Canaan with the people of God. Seven times over in this chapter these nations are mentioned —what God had done to them in the past, how He was prepared to thrust them out, how great a temptation they would be to the people of God if they were allowed to remain, for their presence would inevitably lead to mixed marriages and false worship.

We have said that the book of Joshua is the counterpart of Ephesians in the New Testament. I recall the words of the great Apostle Paul as he stood on the shore at Ephesus saying good-by to the elders of the church: "Take heed therefore unto yourselves, and to all the flock, over which the Holy Spirit has made you overseers, to feed the church of God, which he has purchased with his own blood. For I know this, that after my departing shall grievous wolves enter in among you, not sparing the flock. . . . Therefore watch" (Acts 20:28–31).

There is no level of Christian experience to which any of us may attain from which we may not ultimately go back. We may turn our backs, even in old age, on all the light of the gospel that we have ever received. Oh, the pinnacle from which many Christians have fallen, and the depths to which they have sunk. At any stage of this earthly journey we can account the blood of the covenant wherewith we are sanctified an unholy thing, and do despite to the Spirit of grace. We can throw away all the gathered treasure of spiritual experience of a lifetime, even in the closing stages of this earthly life.

My friends, as we meditate in the presence of God, does not memory sometimes speak to us and recall the promise of former days? Does not memory sometimes bring back vividly to our minds and hearts the bright promise of the springtime of life? Is it not sometimes a tragic contrast to set the memory of life's early years beside the harvest of the fall? Go back twenty years, thirty years, or more, to days of your

adolescence and your young manhood or young womanhood. Think of the promise and hope, think of the dreams
and ambitions that then were yours. Think of the longings
for God, for purity, for holiness—and consider your way
now.

Do we not see in our own hearts today, God forgive us,
the marks of apostasy? Do we not sadly observe the coldness
of our hearts? Do we not meditate sometimes on the prayerlessness of our lives? Are we not conscious sometimes of the
carelessness of our walk with God? Are there not glaring
evidences of neglect and waywardness in the lives of many
of us?

Did we imagine that the battle would become easier as
the years unfolded? Did we believe that youth was the time
of greatest temptation? Did we really think that it was during young manhood and young womanhood that we would
have to fight hardest, that as we got older life would become
less of a struggle? The fact is, we discover that the battle becomes sterner with the passage of the years. Nobody in his
senses would say that anyone determined to go right through
with the purpose of God would ever find the journey easy.
The awful danger of apostasy is in the path of the Christian
every step of the way. How few there are who run well to
the end!

With a deep sense of urgency, almost of fear, I would ask
you, Are there any signs of apostasy in your church today?
Is their any leadership in your church in which the cold,
paralyzing grip of prayerless lives threatens to bring disaster on your fellowship? The passion for souls among you
will soon freeze unless it is supported and led by a dynamic
leadership energized by the Holy Spirit. Is there, then, any

such weak, or indifferent, leadership in your circle, in your church, as I have described? I ask the question in the name of the Lord, and *you* must answer it. Let me ask you now to observe the inevitable results of apostasy.

The first result of apostasy is defeat: "The Lord your God will no more drive out any of these nations from before you" (23:13). There was no question in the mind of Joshua but that every victory had been won by God Himself. Joshua said so in the third verse of this chapter: "Ye have seen what the Lord your God hath done unto all these nations because of you; for the Lord your God is he that hath fought for you."

It is certain that, with the withdrawal of God's power, inevitable defeat will follow, for the evidence of the power of God is given only to those who are faithful to Him. This Pentecostal energy that lifts the church on to a new level of spiritual life is withdrawn from all but an obedient people. Apostasy will lead rapidly to defeat and to resultant dishonor to the name of Christ. "The Lord will no more drive out the enemy."

The second result of apostasy is (in the same verse): discomfort. "They shall be snares and traps unto you, and scourges in your side, and thorns in your eyes." Failure to press on to a full accomplishment of the purposes of God, tolerance of the enemy and willingness to allow him to share the land, will result in desperate discomfort. How often in Christian experience an issue is not really pressed home. How often a sin is not deliberately driven out. How often we see that the temptation we have pampered and encouraged and indulged in has become a scourge and a thorn in our side. The compromising Christian is not a happy man. Let the enemy remain in a Christian life, let him have one foothold. and he soon becomes a scourge.

The third effect of apostasy is disgrace. "Then shall the anger of the Lord be kindled against you, and ye shall perish quickly from off the good land which he hath given unto you" (23:16).

Surely, you ask, there must be safeguards against it? Indeed there are, and Joshua, in his warning of the effects and results of apostasy, was careful to name them to the people of God. In this chapter he proposed three essential safeguards against apostasy.

First of all, obedience. "Be ye therefore very courageous to keep and to do all that is written in the book of the law of Moses, that ye turn not aside therefrom to the right hand or to the left" (23:6). You will recall that the same command was given to Joshua early in life, when he took over leadership from Moses. How true it is that the great principles of our faith are handed down from one generation to another. Every age and every generation of the church are called on to mark, to learn, to inwardly digest the great principles of Christian living, the first of which is obedience.

We say we believe our Bible—thank God that we do! But do we obey? We say we believe it from Genesis to Revelation, but do we live twenty-four hours of the day in the light of its teachings? Have you ever gone to your Bible in your quiet time, and heard God speak to you, and then hurriedly left your quiet time to write a letter, to answer a call, or to speak to your wife, because the Spirit put something on your heart you did not want to face?

Why don't people pray more? Why don't people read their Bibles more? Why don't Christian people today spend

more time alone with God? I can tell you one good reason:
it is too uncomfortable sometimes. For, my friends, as you
turn to the Book, time and time again the Spirit of God will
speak to you about this sin, that habit, your prayerlessness,
your lack of love. He will begin to convince and convict until He has brought you in utter submission to the Saviour.
Failure to obey has caused you to depart altogether from
your quiet time and prayer.

The second great safeguard against apostasy is separation.
Take heed "that you come not among these nations, . . .
neither make mention of the name of their gods, . . . but
cleave unto the Lord your God" (23:7, 8). Of course, that
meant keeping resolutely aloof from all familiar intercourse
with the Canaanites and their sins.

It means the same for the Christian today. It means keeping transparently clear of worldliness. People need to stop
playing at Christianity and really to get down to the battle
against sin and Satan. We excuse ourselves for doing any
worldly thing if we have a nice little devotional talk afterward. God forgive us! What outright hypocrisy! Separation
is a part of the avoidance of apostasy, which means no compromise with the world at all. Of course, that is negative, but
the positive aspect is "cleaving unto the Lord your God."
The separated Christian is not one who gives up things re-
luctantly; the separated Christian is one who loves the Lord
with all his heart and wants nothing else.

Also, how easy it is with the passing of the years to allow
just that little slackness which may not harm you but does
desperate hurt to someone who looks to you for an example.
You may excuse yourself of spending too much time with
your newspaper, too much time with your radio and tele-

vision, by saving, "It won't do me any harm," but it doesn't follow that it doesn't harm those who look to you for leadership and for example in consecrated living. You may say, "It doesn't matter much that I don't come to the prayer meeting. Nobody will miss me." How many young people would say, "It doesn't matter whether I pray—he doesn't go, and I look to him for leadership"?

The third great safeguard against apostasy is the greatest of all. It is this: "Take good heed therefore unto yourselves, that ye love the Lord your God" (23:11). Oh, my friends, failure to obey, failure to maintain standards of separation, can always be traced back to failure in devotion. "If ye love me," said the Lord Jesus, "ye will keep my commandments." Yes, failure to be separated, carelessness in our walk, prayerlessness in our life, can all be traced back to a heart that does not really love our Saviour.

How appropriate are these words, coming at the end of Joshua's life! The earlier years had been full of battle and bloodshed, but now the fighter has become a man of peace. The storm of early years subsides in the sunset, and the man who was always fighting now is saying, "Take heed that ye love."

It all brings to mind that scene on the seashore one day when the Lord Jesus Christ looked Peter through and through and said, "Simon, lovest thou me more than these?" Everything depended on it. Love Christ, and you will be content only if you possess all of Him. Love Him, and you will be bold in your witness. Love Him, and you will love His Book and His law. Love Him, and you will seek no human love that ever could be inconsistent with the love of God. Love Him, and you will possess Him and you will be possessed by Him. Things which otherwise would be scourges and thorns in your side, will be steppingstones to a deeper and fuller experience of His grace and power. Love Him, and you also will love all others who love Him. "Take heed to love."

If I could choose the subject for the last sermon I ever preached, this would be my text. I am quite sure that if the saints of God of past generations could speak in the light of what they have seen of eternity, in the light of what they know of heaven and hell, they would say only these words to us all—"Take heed to love." For the greatest safeguard against carelessness of walk, prayerlessness of spirit, coldness of heart, is love. That which lifts the life of the Christian and of the church on to a new level of fullness of experience, the greatest factor for revival in the church today, is not our advocacy of truth, but the love of our hearts, filled with the Holy Spirit.

Love is of God—God is love. Love alone can conquer discord. Love alone can bind together the divided family of the redeemed. If, therefore, you would love purely and unselfishly and strongly, you must know what it is to love your Saviour. If we would give love, we must first receive love. If we would transmit, we must first absorb. If we would scatter the love of God abroad, we must first have it in our hearts.

The experience of that love in our hearts is through the Holy Spirit, who sheds abroad the love of God. The man who knows love like that has already entered into a corner of heaven; he hungers no more, neither thirsts any more, for he has experienced the fulfillment of the word of Jesus Christ, "The water that I shall give him shall be within him a well of water springing up into everlasting life" (John 4:14).

Yield to the Spirit of God. Never rest until you have completely claimed your share of Pentecost. Remember that the

test of love is not emotion or feeling or speaking, but obey-
ing, for "he that hath my commandments, and keepeth them,
he it is that loveth me" (John 14:21).

Charles Wordsworth's hymn, a paraphrase on part of I
Corinthians 13, brings the message right home to our hearts:

> Gracious Spirit, Holy Ghost,
> Taught by Thee, we covet most
> Of Thy gifts at Pentecost,
>     Holy, heavenly love.
>
> Faith that mountains could remove,
> Tongues on earth or heaven above,
> Knowledge, all things, empty prove
>     Without heavenly love.
>
> Love is kind, and suffers long;
> Love is meek and thinks no wrong;
> Love, than death itself more strong,
>     Therefore give us love.
>
> Prophecy will fade away,
> Melting in the light of day;
> Love will ever with us stay—
>     Therefore give us love.
>
> Faith and hope and love we see
> Joining hand in hand again,
> But the greatest of the three,
>     And the best, is love.
>
> From the overshadowing
> Of thy gold and silver wing,

Shed on us who to Thee cling,
Holy, heavenly love.

Yes, that is the secret—the great safeguard against apostasy —the love of God shed abroad in our hearts by the Holy Spirit (Rom. 5:5).

# CHAPTER 20

# POWER FOR SERVICE

### JOSHUA 24:19

*And Joshua gathered all the tribes of Israel to Shechem, and called for the elders of Israel, and for their heads, and for their judges, and for their officers; and they presented themselves before God.*

*And Joshua said unto all the people, Thus saith the Lord God of Israel, Your fathers dwelt on the other side of the flood in old time, even Terah, the father of Abraham, and the father of Nachor: and they served other gods.*

*And I took your father Abraham from the other side of the flood, and led him throughout all the land of Canaan, and multiplied his seed, and gave him Isaac.*

*And I gave unto Isaac Jacob and Esau: and I gave unto Esau mount Seir, to possess it; but Jacob and his children went down into Egypt.*

*I sent Moses also and Aaron, and I plagued Egypt, according to that which I did among them: and afterward I brought you out.*

*And I brought your fathers out of Egypt: and ye came unto the sea; and the Egyptians pursued after your fathers with chariots and horsemen unto the Red Sea.*

*And when they cried unto the Lord, he put darkness between you and the Egyptians, and brought the sea upon*

*them, and covered them; and your eyes have seen what I
have done in Egypt: and ye dwelt in the wilderness a long
season.*

*And I brought you into the land of the Amorites, which
dwelt on the other side Jordan; and they fought with you:
and I gave them into your hand, that ye might possess their
land; and I destroyed them from before you.*

*Then Balak the son of Zippor, king of Moab, arose and
warred against Israel, and sent and called Balaam the son of
Beor to curse you:*

*But I would not hearken unto Balaam; therefore he blessed
you still: so I delivered you out of his hand.*

*And ye went over Jordan, and came unto Jericho: and the
men of Jericho fought against you, the Amorites, and the
Perizzites, and the Canaanites, and the Hittites, and the Girgashites, the Hivites, and the Jebusites; and I delivered them
into your hand.*

*And I sent the hornet before you, which drave them out
from before you, even the two kings of the Amorites; but
not with thy sword, nor with thy bow.*

*And I have given you a land for which ye did not labour,
and cities which ye built not, and ye dwell in them; of the
vineyards and oliveyards which ye planted not do ye eat.*

*Now therefore fear the Lord, and serve him in sincerity
and in truth: and put away the gods which your fathers
served on the other side of the flood, and in Egypt; and serve
ye the Lord.*

*And if it seem evil unto you to serve the Lord, choose you
this day whom ye will serve; whether the gods which your
fathers served that were on the other side of the flood, or the
gods of the Amorites, in whose land ye dwell: but as for me
and my house, we will serve the Lord.*

*And the people answered and said, God forbid that we should forsake the Lord, to serve other gods;*

*For the Lord our God, he it is that brought us up and our fathers out of the land of Egypt, from the house of bondage, and which did those great signs in our sight, and preserved us in all the way wherein we went, and among all the people through whom we passed:*

*And the Lord drave out from before us all the people, even the Amorites which dwelt in the land: therefore will we also serve the Lord; for he is our God.*

*And Joshua said unto the people, Ye cannot serve the Lord: for he is an holy God; he is a jealous God; he will not forgive your transgressions nor your sins.*

*If ye forsake the Lord, and serve strange gods, then he will turn and do you hurt, and consume you, after that he hath done you good.*

*And the people said unto Joshua, Nay; but we will serve the Lord.*

*And Joshua said unto the people, Ye are witnesses against yourselves that ye have chosen you the Lord, to serve him. And they said, We are witnesses.*

*Now therefore put away, said he, the strange gods which are among you, and incline your heart unto the Lord God of Israel.*

*And the people said unto Joshua, The Lord our God will we serve, and his voice will we obey.*

*So Joshua made a covenant with the people that day, and set them a statute and an ordinance in Shechem.*

JOSHUA 24: 1–25

We come now to the conclusion of these meditations on the book of Joshua. I commenced my ministry in America by emphasizing the teaching of this particular book because within it lies the key which unlocks the door to a new revelation of truth, a deeper experience of spiritual life, and a new anointing for the service of God. Of the need of all of these I was deeply conscious in my own life. I am surer than ever now that the message of full salvation through our union with the Lord Jesus Christ in His death and resurrection, as pictured for us in this book of Joshua, is the greatest need of the church today.

As we come in the closing chapter of this book to Joshua's farewell message to his people, we are not surprised to discover that its theme is service. Every fresh revelation of truth leading to a deeper experience of life must lead to a new anointing for service. So much of our service for God quickly becomes burden and drudgery because it lacks dynamic, and because it is not founded on true revelation of the Word of God. In writing to the Galatians and giving his own testimony, Paul, you remember, said that it pleased God to reveal His Son in him. My friends, the Lord Jesus Christ who did a saving work for us on the Cross must also do a sanctifying work in us by His Spirit, and both of those transactions are equally vital to Christian experience. When truth grips our heart, when it becomes part of our very experience, when we can speak of things that we know, things that we have proved and felt, then Christian service is no longer overwork but overflow.

I want to retrace our steps as we say good-by to this book of Joshua, that we may get a clear picture of the message of the book as a whole. What is the revelation which it unfolds? What is the experience of life that it offers? What is the quality of service that it expects? We shall seek to answer those three questions here; they are summarized for us in the closing chapter of the book.

First, then, what is the revelation that is unfolded in this book of Joshua? If you scan chapter 24 you will find that between verses 2 and 13 the divine personal pronoun occurs no less than seventeen times. Joshua is rehearsing what great things the Lord has done for His people: "I took . . . I gave . . . I sent . . . I brought you out . . . I brought you in . . . I destroyed your enemies . . . I delivered you from the hand of your enemies . . ." As the inspiration for all of the future, Joshua brings to the people the record of their past history. From the very beginning of their history as a nation they owed everything to the intervention and power of almighty God.

That is merely a glimpse of what is clearly taught throughout the whole of the New Testament concerning the salvation which is ours in Jesus Christ our Lord. Confining ourselves just for a moment to the book of Ephesians, which I repeat, is the New Testament commentary on the book of Joshua, notice the second chapter. First, we have *revelation:* "But God, who is rich in mercy, for his great love wherewith he loved us, even when we were dead in sins, hath quickened us together with Christ, (by grace are ye saved;) and hath raised us up together, and made us sit together in heavenly places in Christ Jesus" (Eph. 2:4-6). Then we have *experience:* "That in the ages to come he might shew the exceeding riches of his grace in his kindness toward us through Christ Jesus, for by grace are ye saved, through faith; and that not of yourselves: it is the gift of God: not of works, lest any man should boast" (Eph. 2:7-9). Then, *service:* "For we are his workmanship, created in Christ Jesus unto good works, which God hath before ordained that we should walk in them" (Eph. 2:10). There you have it—revelation, experience, service.

What is that revelation in connection with our life and salvation? Our salvation is all the omnipotent working of God the Father, God the Son, and God the Holy Spirit. God took, He sent, and He gave the Lord Jesus Christ. He brought us out of bondage that He might bring us into the land of blessing. He destroyed our enemies, He delivered us out of their hands—every step of progress in Christian experience has been because of the working of the Holy Spirit. And the over-all, complete plan of that working in your life and mine is to take each of us out of bondage, through the wilderness, into the land of full salvation where we shall know and experience the power of the indwelling Spirit of God to save us from sin. The crowning purpose of the plan is one day to present each one of us perfect before Christ Jesus: perfect in position, accepted in Jesus Christ; and perfect and mature in experience.

Here, then, is the whole revelation of the book. What we are by the grace of God we owe entirely to Him. If there be progress, if there be growth, if there be advance in your Christian life, you owe it all to His indwelling. Everything that we have from God has come to us through His Son by the power of His Spirit—that is the whole revelation of God. You are saved, not because of any act of yours, because of any work of your own, because of any decision that you have made; you are saved because you were chosen in Christ from before the foundation of the world, and one day were convicted of sin by the Holy Spirit, pointed to Calvary; and your heart was opened to the Lord Jesus Christ, and you were born again.

Ever since that day you can record moments of growth

and moments of blessing, all because He who began the good work in you will continue it until the day of Jesus Christ. That is salvation, and when you were saved, that was the beginning of making it real in order that through every sorrow and disappointment, through every joy and blessing, through every testing and trial, you might be made perfect in Christ.

That is the revelation of the book of Joshua; it is the revelation of the whole Word of God.

But let me ask you to notice another revealing experience. In verse 15 we read that Joshua put before the people the choice they must make in the light of all that God had done for them. "Choose you this day," he said, "whom you will serve." The unanimous response of the whole people was to declare their readiness and eagerness to serve the Lord. To that reply Joshua answered somewhat disconcertingly, "Ye cannot serve the Lord your God."

If you think about it for a moment, you will see here a very strange contradiction. On the one hand, God had done everything for the children of Israel. On the other hand, apparently they were utterly unable to do anything for Him in return. Is that true to experience? I suggest to you that it is. How readily have we responded to the claims of Jesus Christ and found ourselves powerless to fulfill our promises! How easily have we vowed that we would do this or that and would go on with God, but when we came to implement that decision (made maybe in the course of a church service) into terms of daily life how helpless have we been to translate it into experience!

In the New Testament, the Lord's Word to His people is also this further revelation, that we are incapable of pleasing Him. "What," says the Apostle Paul, again writing to the

Galatians, "are ye so foolish? having begun in the Spirit, are ye now made perfect by the flesh?" (Gal. 3:3). How frequent have been our failures, how brief our successes! How terribly cold have been our hearts, how changing our emotions! How lacking in real determination have we been through the years of Christian life! Therefore we come to this discovery: that it is possible for a man to have union with Christ, but to be an utter stranger to communion with Him. We may have life, but we may know nothing at all about abundant life. We may pardon, but we may be absolutely powerless over sin. We may be justified, but we may not be sanctified.

The urgent need in the Church of Jesus Christ today is to learn how to deal with the tragic discrepancy between our profession and our experience. For I am persuaded that in Christian living today there is a pathetic difference between what we are in position by virtue of what our Lord did for us on Calvary and what we are in experience by virtue of what He can do in us by the Holy Spirit.

I am suggesting that the prior need for every one of us is to give immediate attention to the discrepancy between justification and sanctification, between being redeemed by the blood and being made holy by the Spirit. The Lord Jesus Christ, who died on the Cross to do a work for us, lives now to work in us by the Spirit, and the innermost significance of true revival in the church is the upsurging of His indwelling life and the outflow of that life in blessing to others. If Christian experience does not rest on revelation, it will be false. If revelation does not lead to Christian experience it will become cold, and we shall lose it.

I remember hearing Dr. Graham Scroggie say on one occasion: "All Christians have eternal life; not all Christians have abundant life. There can be life without health; there can be movement without any progress; there may be war, but defeat. We may serve but never succeed. We may try but never triumph, and the difference all along the line is the difference between possessing life and experiencing life more abundant. This abundant life is simply the fullness of life in Jesus Christ made possible by His death and resurrection, and made real by the incoming of His Spirit. That is abundant life. The trouble with so many of us is that we are on the right side of Easter but the wrong side of Pentecost, the right side of pardon, but the wrong side of power." We are justified, but we are not sanctified. It is not enough to say that we are forgiven; we are called, says the Book, unto holiness.

It is suggested in some quarters that the great trouble in church today is confusion of doctrine in evangelical circles which leads to confusion of experience. I do not believe that. I believe that the great trouble in the church today is a half-and-half salvation with which so many people seem to be perfectly satisfied.

It is illustrated by Israel in the wilderness, between Egypt and Canaan, defeated and in bondage. It is illustrated by Paul's language in Romans 7—the halfway between deliverance from the guilt of sin and freedom from the power of sin. It is illustrated again in I Corinthians 3, in which we have Paul's description of the carnal Christian, in whom there is strife and division but no growth, for he remains a baby. We see the example of it in the life of the early disciples who, between Easter and Pentecost, were gripped with fear and had no real personal sense of vocation. You remember that Peter called them all together and, in a sort of half-hearted, disconsolate, disillusioned voice, said, "I go a-fishing." He had no sense of vocation, no sense of calling, and they were all desperately afraid of what was going to happen to them.

No one can live the life more abundant whose heart is afraid, and who has no real sense of the calling and vocation of God. Time and time again it is deep-rooted conviction of vocation, calling, discipline, that keeps a man through the thick and thin of battle, on the job for Christ all the time. The trouble is that so often in the church today these things are lacking. All of which leads to the tremendous statement which Joshua made to the people of Israel, "Ye cannot serve the Lord your God."

This is the amazing paradox of the Christian life—that although God has done everything for us on the Cross, and waits to do everything in us by the Spirit, we are faced with the appalling fact that we are helpless to make return, "We cannot serve the Lord our God."

But let me ask you, What is the service which God expects from us? Wherein lies the power to realize the experience? I am quite certain that often many of us have been brought to face our absolute helplessness to do anything that is pleasing to the Lord. In spite of all our desire, all our concern, and all our interest in the work, this is written over our experience every day—the utter helplessness of the flesh to do anything which can please Him. On the other hand, we have the offer of a life more abundant, a life that is sanctified and victorious.

How can my helplessness meet God's omnipotence? That is the question we must answer as we finish this study. Too many people have entered by a definite transaction into this deeper life to question the reality of the experience. Too many people have it—too many people have known it—too many people by an experience as real and definite as the day that they were born again have entered into a life more abundant and stepped out of the wilderness into the land for the truth to be challenged.

Dwight L. Moody once said in Glasgow,—I quote his words: "One day in New York—oh, what a day! I cannot describe it; I seldom refer to it. It is almost too sacred an experience to name. I can only say God revealed Himself to me, and I had such an experience of His love that I had to ask Him to stay His hand. I went to preaching again; the sermons were no different. I did not present any new truth, and yet hundreds were converted. I would not be placed back where I was before that blessed experience if you would give me all Glasgow." Moody entered in by a definite transaction with God to a new and deeper life on a totally different level.

David Brainerd, as it is recorded in his biography, was wet with sweat and almost overcome as he grasped at God for the souls before him, but he so preached that scores of stoic, hard-hearted Indian people were bowed down like grass before a scythe.

Home in England for new recruits after years on the mission field, Hudson Taylor sat in contemplation one day and became conscious as never before of his helplessness and unworthiness and uselessness in the service of God, when, to quote his own words, he recognized that "it is not what Hudson Taylor does for God that matters, but what God does through Hudson Taylor." And from that day he commenced to live what he called the "exchanged life," in which it was "no more *I*, but Christ."

You say to me, "These men are giants of the faith, they are exceptions; such an experience is not for me." They became giants only because they obeyed God. Satan blinds the minds of Christian people to the reality of this and makes them content with a half-and-half salvation. These men became giants only because they obeyed God, waited on Him, claimed what He had promised in His Book. If they are exceptions, what a tragic commentary on the rest of us! God has no favorites, but He has an experience for us as high and different from the average Christian level of the wilderness life as conversion was above the life that you lived before you were saved. We need not wait for God—He is waiting for us. Joshua said to his people, "Now, therefore, put away the strange gods that are among you, and incline your hearts unto the Lord God of Israel" (24:23).

I hesitate here to say any word of personal testimony, for it may sound like spiritual pride, but God knows my heart. I remember the day the Lord faced me with this very truth, and I knew that there were idols in my life as a preacher that had to go. One was the idol of the tobacco pouch; others were idols of affections that were out of God's will. There was an idol of unyielded money, of no discipline in giving. There was the idol of the sharp tongue of criticism that refused to admit into fellowship brethren who did not exactly agree with what I thought about the Bible. There was the idol of a cold heart, the idol therefore of a comparatively prayerless life. I remember the day when God just broke me down because of these idols.

I would not say that I am perfect. Indeed, I blush to think of the many times I have failed since then, but I have come to see and feel, on a deeper level every day, that this more abundant life is offered to me, not as a final step, but as an initial crisis which leads to a process. I discover every day that there is more and more of Jesus if I would press on with God and be hungry for all that He has for me in Christ.

There is no such thing as a final experience of claiming Him by faith, but then, as you go on with God, that experience enlarges as your capacity increases, your life becomes greater, and your self becomes smaller, and Jesus Christ becomes the altogether lovely One.

Therefore, if we would serve, we must first surrender. If we would overcome, we must first obey. For service is much more than mere ceremony, it is bowing the heart before the majesty of God in Jesus Christ. It is the transformation of our character into a reflection of His purity, it is the approach of a needy, unholy one to God, the Holy One, by merit of the sacrifice that was made on Calvary's tree. It is the discovery that sanctification is achieved and holiness is won and experienced in exactly the same way as that in which I was justified. It is all of faith. It is not my struggle to attain it, it is not my effort to strive after purity and godliness, it is to receive by faith all that there is of Jesus to be personally to me all that He offers to be to us all.

What a day it is going to be when we acknowledge our failure, and in spite of it still believe that we can yet become all that is in the will of God to make us! Jesus Christ offers Himself to you as the source of all strength and all power. You have tried, but have failed. Why not begin trusting? You have tried in your own strength, and you have found it weakness. Why not take hold of His power? But if you would do that, you must be ready to forsake. Must we cling to worldly things and practice them in order to make worldly people think that, after all, Christians are only human? I think not. If you would enter into the life more abundant, then test everything you do by your love for the Lord Jesus Christ. Let nothing dim your view of Calvary.

Augustine once said, as a principle of his life, "To myself I will show a heart of steel, to my fellow-man a heart of love, to my God a heart of flame." This is the quality of service and life for which God is calling from each of us, His children. That is the service and the experience offered to you, based on the revelation of the Book.

"Choose you *this day* whom ye will serve; . . . but as for me and my house, we will serve the Lord" (24:15).